The Turned Card

The Turned Card

Christianity before and after the Wall

Desmond O'Grady

"Now the card of history has been turned."
– Metropolitan Andrey Sheptytsky

 Loyola Press

Loyola Press
3441 North Ashland Avenue
Chicago, Illinois 60657

First Published in 1995
Gracewing
Fowler Wright Books
Southern Avenue, Leominster
Herefordshire HR6 0QF
England

O'Grady, Desmond, 1929–
      The turned card : Christianity before and after the wall /
Desmond O'Grady ; foreword by Andrew M. Greeley.
      p.   cm.
      Originally published: Leominster, Herefordshire : Gracewing,
1995.
      Includes index.
      ISBN 0-8294-0938-6
      1. Christianity—Europe, Eastern—History—20th century.
2. Communism and Christianity—Europe, Eastern. I. Title.
[BR738.6.028   1997]
274.7'0829—dc21   96-52196
                                                          CIP

Cover design by Ginny Pitre-Hay

97 98 99 00 01 / 10 9 8 7 6 5 4 3 2 1

Contents

Foreword

Desmond O'Grady has written the best and most sophisticated book available in English on religion in Europe before and after the collapse of the Socialist empire—story of the lights and shadows, the successes and the failures, the hopes and the disappointments of the tumultuous years as the impossible happened: Communism collapsed and religion became free again.

The brightest of the pictures in his story are of religious leaders in various countries allying themselves with the brave men and women who broke down the walls in their countries in a heroic quest for freedom. The most promising pictures are of the resurgence of religion in many of the countries, most notably Russia itself. The darkest of the pictures are of Church leaders more interested in their own institutional power than the rights and freedoms of their people. The most discouraging pictures are of Church leaders antagonizing their own people (especially in Poland) by their attempts to impose their own authoritarian controls on the newly free people.

It is too early to say what will happen to religion in Eastern Europe. Certainly the resurgence of Orthodoxy in Russia and Bulgaria seems to be durable, despite the obduracy of some of the Orthodox leaders. Poles will remain Catholics, of course, but now on their own terms like Catholics in the West. The reader must judge what will develop in the long run out of the trends which O'Grady so vividly describes.

Andrew Greeley, Chicago

Feast of All Souls, 1996

Acknowledgments

Thanks are due to all those interviewed and to the following for their advice: Father Edmund Campion; Father Mark Coleridge; George Damborg; Philip Gudgeon; Borys Gudziak; M-C Hubert; John Long, S.J.; Padre Sergio Mercanzin; Gerald O'Collins, S.J.; Monsignor Franc Rode, C.M.; Antanas Saulaitis, S.J.; Ed Schmidt, S.J., for his meticulous editing; Boguslaw Steczek, S.J.; and Diethard Zils, O.P.

Chapter 1

From Euphoria to Amnesia

In the euphoria that followed the fall of the Berlin Wall, who could have foreseen that within seven years Poland's Ex-President-without-a-Pension Lech Wałęsa would, between lecture tours abroad, attempt to resume his job as an electrician at the shipyard in Gdansk, which was near bankruptcy? Or that, on Pope John Paul's arrival in Vilnius, Lithuania, on September 4, 1993, Algirdas Brazauskas would greet him as president? Overwhelmingly, Catholic Lithuania had preferred a former Communist, albeit one who had taken up the nationalist cause, to Vytautas Landsbergis, who symbolized the Lithuanian nationalists' struggle for independence.

Brazauskas was not an isolated figure: ex-Communists won most votes in the Polish elections held that same month, as they did in the Hungarian elections in May 1994. Elsewhere, throughout Central and Eastern Europe, ex-Communists held key political and economic positions. In most cases, it was not that the Lithuanian, Polish, and Hungarian electors wanted the old Communism, but neither did they want what had replaced it. In October 1996, however, Vytautas Landsbergis's party won the Lithuanian elections. Some claimed the result was a harbinger of a widespread swing of the pendulum against ex-Communists. Whether or not this forecast proved accurate, it was positive that governments were being changed without violence. Nevertheless the difficulties being experienced in the 90s raised the

1

question of whether it had been a mere illusion to believe that the implosion of Communism meant that the card of history had turned—and not only for Central and Eastern Europe.

It was not surprising that John Paul II welcomed the abrupt and nonviolent end of the atheistic Communist system as "God's victory." From his viewpoint, the events of 1989–90 seemed not so much current affairs as a chapter of salvation history. But what had seemed the best of times was swiftly followed by the worst of presages because of economic problems and truculent nationalisms. The Bosnian conflict illustrated the possibility of ghastly ethnic-nationalist clashes.

Indeed, when the Iron Curtain was raised, some Western Europeans discovered Easterners to be like a long-awaited relative who is desperately poor, unpredictable, full of atavistic resentments, and capable of wrecking the shared home. Each ethnic group seemed to want its own state, but even many Germans found cohabitation with other Germans irksome: some claimed that a rebuilt Berlin Wall would have been a boon.

After the fall of the Wall, amnesia tended to replace euphoria. The experience of the Communist years was being forgotten before its implications had been explored. But journalistic assignments in Central and Eastern Europe over the past twenty-five years and longer coverage of Vatican affairs prompted my interest in questions such as to what degree post-Wall problems, including increased Catholic-Orthodox tensions, were legacies of the Communist era. How did Christians live under Communism; who were their heroes? Have they adapted to the changed circumstances of the 1990s, and what is involved in rebuilding the Christian Churches? Will reestablishment of Church structures stifle the initiative shown during the resistance to Communism? Above all, what can the almost 200 million Christians (100 million Orthodox, 70 million Catholics, and 20 million Protestants) do to ensure that the joy which exploded throughout Central Europe in 1989–90 was not a mere illusion?

Chapter 2

Sighs of the Soul

The Berlin Wall collapsed under countless sighs: sighs for democracy, sighs for color, excitement, and things that could not be bought, and sighs for religion as suggested by the phrase "religion is the . . . spirit of spiritless conditions." The spiritless, oppressive world that Communism had created did not resist the needs of souls whose existence it had denied.

Originally, "religion is the . . . spirit of spiritless conditions" had criticized heartless capitalism in which religion was often seen as the alibi of an unjust status quo. This viewpoint was in line with the conviction of some representatives of the Enlightenment that religion served simply to keep the lower orders in their place. The corollary was that, if there were to be social justice, religion had to be destroyed. Indeed, it was in his introduction to *The Critique of Hegel's Philosophy of Right* that Karl Marx had written: "Religion is the sigh of oppressed creatures, the sentiment of a heartless world, and the spirit of spiritless conditions."

In *My Country Right or Left,* George Orwell, commenting approvingly on Marx's words, wrote: "Religious belief, in the form in which we had known it, had to be abandoned." He acknowledged, however, that when the soul is amputated, the wound has a tendency to go septic, as had been shown by the horrors of the modern world, including those of "Marxist realism." Although this proved a huge septic wound, Orwell's response was not rejuvenated religion but

3

belief in human brotherhood without need of a "life to come" to give it meaning. He ignored Dostoyevsky's "if God does not exist, all evil is permissible" and could not foresee the testimony of many such as fiction writer Varlam Shalamov, who was to write: "In the gulags, I did not see anyone who had more dignity than believers. Everyone's soul was degraded, only believers resisted." Nor did Orwell foresee the Polish Solidarity movement, which was partly inspired by Catholic social doctrine and which was to show that conflict between religion and social justice is not inevitable.

Marx's criticism that religion is a sop for the suffering of the poor applied particularly to the Russian Orthodox Church, which at times was little more than an instrument of state power. This was relevant elsewhere also: Tadeusz Mazowiecki, the first post-Communist Polish prime minister, wrote that "at least at the beginning, Socialism was the guilty conscience of Christianity" (in Poland, as throughout the former Austro-Hungarian Empire, the Catholic Church had had strong links with the wealthy and a stake in maintaining an unjust status quo). To many, Communism had seemed the way to utilize scientific progress to eliminate social injustice, but in the euphoria over the end of European Communism, the reasons for its initial success were often overlooked. World War I and the Depression had seemed to confirm the historical inevitability of Communism's advance: they were interpreted by many as the death throes of capitalism. Communism was attractive to many people also because of its opposition to various forms of fascism, some of which had a religious coloring.

In the event, democratic capitalism was to prove more resourceful than Communism. Western Christianity did not blindly bless profit-makers: from Leo XIII (1878–1903) onwards, the Catholic Church rejuvenated its teaching on social justice and denounced the shortcomings not only of Communism but also of capitalism. In England, the Wesleyan

Chapel was a formative influence on the Labour movement. In the United States and Australia, reformist Democratic and Labour parties were largely influenced by Catholic immigrants. Social involvement helped Western Christianity to retain relevance, although the Orthodox might claim that it thereby loosened its links with transcendence.

Russian Orthodox identification with czarism, however, made transcendence seem merely evasion, religion a means of social control, and atheism a liberation from hypocrisy. Marxism promised that new social relations, by eliminating exploitation and alienation, would lead to the demise of religion. This outcome could be accelerated by propagating atheism (in the Soviet Union through campaigns of the League of the Godless) and repressing superstition (used as a synonym of religious practices). The hated metaphysical human person had to be crushed.

Marxism-Leninism's allegedly scientific insight into the workings of history was supposed to guarantee that the Party would introduce a reign of justice. The present and the people it comprised could be sacrificed to a radiant future. Ending what Marx called "man's exploitation by man" was an admirable goal, but harnessing class hatred to achieve it produced a parody of social justice.

Gradually, Communist idealists were disillusioned. The Montenegrin writer-politician Milovan Djilas explained that he had become a Communist because of his dissatisfaction with society and a "religious impulse to believe in a better world." But by the mid-1950s Djilas protested that Communism, far from producing equality, put society in the hands of a new class of privileged people, the nomenklatura. He called Communism "industrial feudalism" and lamented that "the Revolution has given me everything except satisfaction for my deepest aspirations."

Communism remained in power and Communist attitudes and reflexes persisted for, as one Muscovite said, "they seep through us like nicotine"; but by the 1970s there were fewer convinced Communists. According to an article in *La Nuova Europa* (March–April 1993) by Archbishop Mario Rizzi, the Apostolic Nuncio in Bulgaria, when in March 1978 Karol Wojtyła came from Cracow to Rome to preach the Lenten sermons to Paul VI, he said that the game was up, that there should not be excessive worry about Communism because it was finished.

Communist regimes considered Christianity a mere survival of a fading order; but after failing to crush it entirely they tried instead to preserve it in mummified form until the babushkas (grandmothers) died off and also as a cultural "showpiece" for foreigners. But Communism, rather than Christianity, was the mummy. Christianity showed surprising vitality, representing the only alternative worldview to official ideology and the only structures and spaces where free discussions could take place. When, increasingly, people found it tiresome, as Václav Havel wrote, "to live a lie," Christian insistence that Christ was the Truth became more compelling. Communism predicated a new human person, but the only persuasive exemplars were dedicated Christians. The Second Vatican Council had encouraged greater social involvement, and Christians began to reinterpret Marxist terms such as "alienation." Christians provided models of community to replace the Communist husk, attracting both non-Christian young people and more than a sprinkling of intellectuals: in Poland, Adam Michnik acknowledged that "the Church teaches us all that we may bow only before God" and recognized that the Gospel had championed social justice long before Marx. Michnik was one of the many secular intellectuals who allied with Christians in defense of human rights.

Among other allies were environmentalists who were angered that Central and Eastern Europe was polluted as well as poor: writers such as Mikhail Bulgakov, Czesław Miłosz, and Aleksandr Solzhenitsyn, who proposed values which brought censorship of their works; those who fought for human rights in

East Germany, Poland, Czechoslovakia, and Hungary; indeed, all who refused to acquiesce in demeaning compromise.

. Like Christians, Jews were disadvantaged, but it was because of their race as well as their religion. There was little collaboration between the two groups: not only were they diffident of one another, but many feared collaboration would increase repression. The collaboration between them, which took place in the Solidarity movement or through people such as Elena Bonner, the wife of Andrei Sakharov, was on a basis different from religion.

Some Communists saw the need for reform. The Soviet Communist Party Central Committee recognized a social as well as an economic crisis and in 1986 appointed Mikhail Gorbachev to make the changes necessary to avoid their getting out of control. Gorbachev's book *Perestroika* (restructuring) showed that he was so convinced of the validity of socialism that he mistakenly believed the Party could retain consensus without the backing of force or fear. The military budget imposed an impossible burden but Gorbachev did not recognize economic necessities or the extent of nationalistic resentment against Soviet rule. He unleashed the *glasnost* (transparency) genie, which showed change was urgent, but with time people became convinced that the government did not intend to bring it about. Moreover Gorbachev wanted to discredit Stalin while saving Lenin, but it was not possible to distinguish between them so sharply.

When the aging "dinosaurs" who ruled the satellite countries appealed for help against those pushing for changes, Gorbachev did not prop them up. Revocation of the Brezhnev Doctrine of limited sovereignty deprived regimes of the Red Army's backing. There seem to be grounds for the claim that the K.G.B. and its counterpart organizations in the satellite countries acquiesced in the ousting of the old guard, hoping that Gorbachev clones would replace it. But the renewal movement could not be controlled.

The English historian Timothy Garton Ash has stated that the economic crisis was a "necessary, but by no means sufficient, cause of the revolution. The decisive causes can be found in the realm of conscience."

Chinese and Vietnamese Communist Party officials also seemed to be aware of the realm of conscience, because after the collapse of European Communism they warned against the subversive effects of religion. At a Chinese Communist Party Congress in December 1989, officials held John Paul II responsible for liberalization in the Soviet Bloc.

Mikhail Gorbachev wrote in the Turin daily *La Stampa* that the changes in Central and Eastern Europe could not have occurred without John Paul. Certainly, the pope dramatized the problems on the international scene. Former Polish president General Wojciech Jaruzelski has suggested that the beginning of the end for Communism was the papal trip to Poland in 1979: "He gave impulse to the birth of Solidarity and Wałęsa and from there . . ."

Timothy Garton Ash confirmed Jaruzelski's assessment: "I do believe that the Pope's first great pilgrimage to Poland was the turning point [which triggered the collapse of Communism]. Here, for the first time, we saw that large-scale, substantial, yet supremely peaceful and self-disciplined manifestation of social unity, of gentle crowd against party-State, which was both the hallmark and the essential domestic catalyst of change in 1989 . . . The Pope's visit was followed, just over a year later, by the birth of Solidarity and without the Pope's visit it is doubtful if there would have been a Solidarity."

But although Poland showed that changes could occur, they came about differently in each country. This is not to deny that the breakthrough which came in Poland sent shockwaves through European Communism. But there were other factors at work also.

For instance, although Catholics played a greater part in the demise of the Communist regime in Albania than their 10 percent of the population would suggest, their influence was not comparable to that of Catholics in Poland, and there was no counterpart to the Solidarity movement.

An even more cogent example of the diverse ways in which countries liberated themselves from Communism and of the limits of the John Paul–Solidarity influence, is provided by Lithuania which borders Poland and has almost as high a proportion of Catholics. The Lithuanian Catholic Church played the major role in preserving believers' freedoms and human rights and in maintaining national identity. Indirectly it shaped the resistance movement, in which Catholics were prominent. But while this confirms the important role that religion played in resisting totalitarianism, it does not confirm the "Jericho syndrome" or the "John Paul did it all" thesis. One factor in its difference from Poland is that Lithuania was part of the Soviet Union and was thus tightly controlled and sealed off almost hermetically. Another factor is that between the first and second world wars, Vilnius, the Lithuanian capital, had been part of Poland, and this caused continuing bad feeling. Lithuanian distrust of Poland and hostility to its resident Poles inhibited exchanges. In fact, Solidarity had more contact with Czechoslovakian dissidents than with Lithuanian.

In Timişoara, Romania, the parishioners of a Reformed minister, Lazlo Tökes, reacted against security police when they attempted to evict him. This sparked an uprising which led to the fall of the regime of Romanian President Nicolae Ceauşescu. This case, with its mixed ethnic and religious motives, well illustrated the claim of Józef Tischner, a priest-philosopher in Cracow, that "the Christian affirmation of transcendence implies a need for liberty which prevents people accepting totalitarianism."

Although many members of the Evangelical Church of East Germany, the largest denomination with 4.5 million faithful, had collaborated with the regime, towards the end of the 1980s it attracted those interested in dissenting from official policy on human rights, disarmament, and environmental protection.

Likewise in Lviv, Ukraine, those who threw their military conscription cards into a tub in the main square, whether religious or not, joined religious manifestations which challenged the status quo.

In Czechoslovakia in the latter half of the 1980s, tens of thousands found the courage to participate in religious processions partly because they were devout, partly because they were defiant. Christian celebrations brought tens of thousands together, vanquishing the fear which was the regime's cement.

But claims for Christianity's role in Communism's collapse can be exaggerated: Christians endured and Communism caved in, but it was not a simple cause-and-effect relationship. Christians were temporarily allied with other groups against regimes which evaporated once their leaders had a change of heart or lost their nerve. The streetcar which traversed the Wall was named Desire for Something Else and its passengers got off at different stops.

Christianity survived Communism with a high prestige that gave it great potential for the post-Communist era. Those who underestimate this potential also often fail to realize the influence of Christians and the consequences of their World War II experience in Western Europe. The shared resistance to Nazism in Western Europe helped to break down barriers between denominations and between Christians and others. Among Christians, this encouraged ecumenism and a new openness to contemporary culture which bore fruit in the Second Vatican Council. It also prompted Catholic politicians such as Robert Schuman in France, Alcide De Gasperi in Italy, and Konrad Adenauer in West Germany to look beyond old enmities and old frontiers to forge the European community. World War II ended in Central and Eastern Europe only in 1989, and bridge-building has been slower there than in the West.

The situation in post-Communist Europe differs significantly from that of postwar Western Europe. The United States, which played a major role in Western Europe's recovery, is providing only about 20 percent of the aid in formerly Communist Europe; Western Europe supplies the remainder. Although much of Western Europe was destroyed by World War II, Ireland, Spain, Portugal, Sweden, and Switzerland did not participate, while the United Kingdom was not overrun. Communism, however, dominated all of Central and Eastern Europe, where many countries had previously been debilitated by subjection to Nazi Germany. Moreover, Communist domination lasted four decades (seven in the case of the USSR) as against the five years of Nazism in Western Europe outside Germany. In many Western countries, future leaders were formed in the resistance movement, but there was little comparable in much of Communist Europe as the regimes had lasted decades and then changed very rapidly. Furthermore, as Czesław Miłosz and others have shown, in Communist Europe successive generations of the brightest were harassed, while those who toed the party line were promoted. In some countries, Christians were excluded from the universities; in others they were excluded from the university humanities faculties because philosophical concepts were at issue. Postwar Western Europe did not face problems comparable to the Bosnian conflict. There are abundant reasons, then, for the slow recovery in Central and Eastern Europe.

The most striking difference between Christians in the West after World War II and in post-Communist Europe is that, whereas in Western Europe many collaborated against totalitarianism, in Central and Eastern Europe the Orthodox Church had benefited from Stalin's suppression of Eastern-rite Catholic Churches. In Romania, two Catholic bishops died while held in Orthodox monasteries. There are historical reasons, if not justifications, for the Orthodox attitudes, which will be discussed later. But certainly cases of Orthodox collaboration with the oppressors have blighted hopes for post-Communist Christian ecumenism and has reduced Christianity's potential. During the Synod of Bishops in the Vatican in December 1991, John Paul II deplored the scandal of Christians divided in a Europe moving towards political union.

At the synod, some participants were compared to those from the Nubian province who, in 325 A.D., attended the first ecumenical council in Nicaea bearing the scars of Diocletian's persecution. But the change in the Roman Empire when Constantine chose Christianity has not been paralleled by that in Central and Eastern Europe. Constantine encouraged Christianity by building churches at his own expense, aiding the clergy, and modifying laws. These innovations, coming immediately after the most severe persecution, gave him perhaps an unfortunately strong hand vis-à-vis the Church; but it was a helping hand. There is no comparable ruler in the post-Communist Europe, which at least reduces the likelihood of opportunistic conversions such as occurred under Constantine.

What is comparable is the postpersecution confusion: the aftermath of persecution can be nearly as damaging as persecution itself. One reason for this at the time of the Roman Empire was that those who courageously witnessed to their beliefs acquired an authority greater than that of established ecclesiastical office-holders. This time around, the possibility of contrast between charisma and ecclesiastical office was reduced when strong witnesses were made cardinals (Miloslav Vlk of the Czech Republic, Ján Korec of Slovakia, Alexandru Todea of Romania, Kazimierz Swiatek of Belarus, and Mikel Koliqi of Albania).

A further postpersecution problem familiar from the first centuries is the need to clear up ambiguous situations created by those who compromised or who, under pressure, committed administrative irregularities. One example is the case of clandestine Czech priests who married during the Communist regime and, after it, wanted recognition from the Vatican. (In

1996 a new Eastern-rite exarchate with its own bishop was founded into which some married priests were incorporated, as is accepted in the Eastern-rite Catholic Church.) The qualities needed to resist persecution can sometimes become a drawback once it ceases. Moreover, under prolonged oppression the faith of some deepens but that of others atrophies: the whole concern of Christians can become the preservation of the faith passed on as if in an envelope. This produces believers who, after persecution, are disinclined to dialogue, even with coreligionists from outside.

The witness of heroic Christians convinced some that once Communism collapsed a light from the East would spiritually revivify the West. This has not occurred. There had been a miracle: that Christianity survived at all. Shortly before his death in 1990 at the age of ninety-four, the Latvian Cardinal Julijans Vaivods remarked that Christ had promised the gates of hell would not prevail against the Church, but nothing more—hell's gates could come within a hair's breadth of prevailing. Communism not only destroyed Church institutions that for centuries had been the basis of some countries' culture and of their educational and hospital systems, but it also prevented installation of Christian churches and schools during extensive urbanization. Sustained state hostility and atheistic education took their toll: as a result, many acquired only scant acquaintance with Christian practices, and often those who considered themselves Christians had only rudimentary beliefs. Some Christians suffered more than others. In Poland, Yugoslavia, and East Germany, despite restrictions, parishes and religious orders continued to function. But where repression was total, many lived their faith in secret.

While Christians were suffering for their beliefs, the Vatican was attempting to help them by negotiating with Communist regimes. An analysis will be made later of this controversial policy, John Paul II's impact on it, his vision of Europe, and his assessments, during visits to post-Communist Central and

Eastern Europe, of the prospects for rebuilding both the Christian Churches and society.

In this work the term "underground Church" is used, but a Czech priest, Tomáš Halík, has pointed out that it was invented by state internal security forces who hoped to play an underground Church off against the official Catholic Church. He added that the Czech security forces may have imagined there was a centrally directed underground Church, but instead it consisted of groups of priests and laity without coordination or, often, even without contact between them.

Halík, who prepared for the priesthood in secret and was ordained on a weekend trip to East Germany, prefers to speak of concealed or unofficial priests not divided in the Church from those with whom they often collaborated. The unofficial priests supplemented the work of official or publicly active priests, for instance by preparing candidates for baptism, first communion, and other sacraments. In both categories, there were both worthy and unworthy priests. But, as John Paul said in the Prague cathedral, there was only one Church.

Halík identifies three groups. There were regularly trained, officially ordained priests who had a state license but then lost it and were usually imprisoned for a time. Most did not receive a license again—although some did during the brief period of Alexander Dubček's leadership—but continued to minister in secret. Miloslav Vlk, who became archbishop of Prague on March 27, 1991, was one of these. A second group were those ordained by foreign bishops, including Karol Wojtyła of Cracow. Their qualifications were carefully examined and their ordinations were approved by the Holy See; many belonged to religious orders. Halík was of this group. Most of the post-Communist problems arose with a third group, whose preparation for the priesthood was often clandestine and sketchy and who were ordained, without the Holy See's prior approval, by local bishops who had themselves been secretly ordained.

These distinctions applied in Czechoslovakia and Hungary, where the state licensed priests. In Ukraine and Romania, the Eastern-rite Catholic Churches were absorbed by the Orthodox. As officially the Churches no longer existed, all their faithful were "underground." Many of their priests, if not imprisoned, had other occupations but in secret continued their ministry, usually administering sacraments in homes or in the woods. Some of their bishops were ordained without the Holy See's being able to check on them, and they in turn ordained priests who had not lived in a seminary and had studied only as best they could.

Some Westerners admire the Church of Silence as one which never raised awkward theological questions, but this was probably because, although morally strong, it was not in a position to be intellectually adventurous. When the Vatican brought the worker-priest experiment to a halt in France in 1954, priests in Central and Eastern Europe were working in factories not as an experiment with a slightly artificial air but as a necessity. The French worker-priests were gesturing towards the working class, but in Communist societies there was a proletariat of priests. These experiences, along with the collective memory of the suffering in a society without God, provide a basis for future developments which will differ from those in the West.

It is mistaken to romanticize Christians' behavior under Communism, and it is unnecessary. Some humanists found ethical reasons to resist while some Christians crumbled. But under inhuman pressure, Christians proved humanity's best resource. The following chapter consists of stories, gleaned mainly on trips to Central and Eastern Europe, of Christians who, by preserving their interior freedom under Communism, pointed beyond it. Most of the stories are pursued only until Communism evaporated; some are resumed later, when it will be seen that not all concerned had the flexibility needed in post-Communist societies. The settings for their resistance were as diverse as Kazakhstan and Slovakia, and the circumstances differed considerably, but each made a choice and constantly reaffirmed it. All believed in something other than what John Paul II called Communism's "tragic utopia." And all tended to share their faith, to form a community.

Catholic priests traversed the steppes of Soviet Asia to serve communities of deported Germans, Poles, and other nationalities. Their wanderings combined religious zeal with a taste for adventure: they were virtually freelancers, because bishops were so distant. Some Orthodox, mainly young, university-trained laity in European Russia, challenged not only the atheist state but also their own bishops' collusion with the K.G.B. As most had a Communist upbringing, their choice foreshadowed a religious rebirth. It should be noted that some of these Orthodox spoke in favor of oppressed Catholics in West Ukraine. Christians who resisted Communism seemed isolated, but, at great distances, they recognized brothers and sisters, even of other denominations and races. This vision is needed in ex-Communist Europe as an antidote to intolerant ethnicity. The stories of these Christians not only preserve a memory but also provide hope.

It is a hope more exalted than Orwell's—echoed decades later by John Lennon's "Imagine"—for a "brotherhood of man" without religion, but his vision will attract those who see religion only as a stimulus for strife, for ethnic enmities.

Perhaps religion goes together with the will to live or die for something or, rather, someone. "In the twentieth century nobody dies for their faith," said General Alexandru Nicolski of the Rumanian Securitate police, when interrogating Alexandru Todea. But Nicolski was mistaken. The belief that there are things worth dying for—and the courage to affirm them—was the glory of Christians in Communist Europe.

Chapter 3

Strong in the Faith

Before presenting contemporary Christians who have been strong in the faith, it is worth recalling some of the Church leaders who symbolize Catholic resistance to Communism. Four cardinals come immediately to mind: the Pole, Stefan Wyszyński; the Czech, Jozef Beran; the Hungarian, József Mindszenty; and the Croat, Alojzije Stepinac. All were imprisoned by the Communists, and Beran and Mindszenty had received the same treatment from the Nazis. Stepinac and Mindszenty may have opposed the Communists for mixed motives, but all four steadfastly refused to bow to attempts to crush the Church. Photographs of Mindszenty on trial, his eyes in a chalky face huge with fear and, perhaps, the after-effects of will-weakening drugs, came to stand for all those subjected to trials which were simply legalized vendetta. Stepinac, Mindszenty, and Beran were removed from their dioceses, but Wyszyński weathered all the storms and lived to see his fellow Pole, Karol Wojtyła, become Pope John Paul II on October 16, 1978. Wyszyński embodied the Church Suffering, the Church Militant, and the Church Triumphant.

In their former dioceses, procedures to ascertain whether Wyszyński, Mindszenty, and Stepinac should be canonized began in 1994. But it is another leader of the Catholic resistance, the Bulgarian Eugheni Bossilkov (1900–52), who was the first Catholic bishop–victim of Communism after World War II whose beatification was approved.

One of four children of a farming family which lived in a Danube village, he entered a minor seminary of the Passionist order when eleven and three years later left for a decade of studies with the Passionists in Holland and Belgium, where he acquired a taste for cigars and drinking Bols. In 1926 he returned home for ordination, then the following year went to Rome for studies at the Pontifical Oriental Institute. A Latin-rite priest, he had excellent relations with Bulgarian Orthodox.

In 1932 he became responsible for a parish in the Danube plain. Ebullient Bossilkov was a sportsman and hunter, a good tenor and an organist who formed a parish choir. A persuasive preacher, he interested youth in the faith.

In 1944 the Red Army invaded Bulgaria and helped the small Communist Party overturn the monarchy. The fighting and the purges which followed resulted in over 100,000 deaths. "Our sufferings came after the war," wrote Bossilkov to Dutch friends. He corresponded with two "aunts" in Holland who had financed his studies and also with a Catholic couple he had known; he reminded his aunts how, with other seminarians, he used to arrive by bicycle at their house and "rob" plums from their garden.

In 1945 Bossilkov was made apostolic administrator of Nikopol and the following year bishop. He authorized a mission (a cycle of homilies to revivify the faith) throughout the diocese which was disturbed by Communists publicly challenging the preacher. Bossilkov felt he was under constant surveillance. "I've some guardian angels," he joked, "but St. Michael doesn't know about them." His niece, a nun, has said that he was convinced the regime wanted to detach the Church in Bulgaria from the Pope and attempted to enlist him by offering a villa, a car, and much money if he would establish a national Catholic Church.

In 1948 the government began to close Catholic institutions. There were 3 Catholic bishops, 55,000 Latin-rite Catholics, plus 10,000 of the Eastern-rite. They sustained a

Catholic publishing house and a weekly newspaper; two hospitals and a tuberculosis clinic; orphanages; nine secondary schools, many primary schools, kindergartens; and two seminaries. Catholic schools were closed and the government threatened a new, more restrictive law on religion. In this tense situation, Bossilkov somehow received permission to visit his "aunt"-benefactors in Holland and go to Rome on his way back.

One evening another Passionist found him praying in the Basilica of St. Mary Major in Rome: Bossilkov explained that he needed the grace to die as a martyr for his diocese. Others recounted similar episodes that suggest he foresaw his fate but was seeking the courage to face it; to those who suggested that he should not return, he said he had to die among his clergy and people. Bossilkov felt he was spied upon even in Rome. After an audience with Pius XII he returned home. By now Church activities were largely confined to the celebration of Mass, but nevertheless the young bishop carried out pastoral visits.

The Protestant community, even smaller than the Catholic, was crushed after fifteen pastors were arrested and condemned to long prison terms for alleged spying. After this, the Communist authorities demanded that the Catholic bishops testify that there was religious liberty. They sent a telegram to the Australian Herbert Evatt, who was president of the United Nations: "Until now our churches are open, the faithful can accede freely to them and to religious ceremonies. Religious liberty is regulated by the law on Religious Associations." Bossilkov foresaw that the Communists would demand more.

Earlier, in February, he had written to the head of the Dutch Passionists: "I'm preparing for the worst . . . If one day you hear it [the worst news], continue praying and the stains of our blood will open the road to a splendid future." He added that he had decided the foreign missionaries, who constituted half the priests in his diocese, should leave. "Here the difficulties are becoming enormous. I can't say what I feel, which means I'm on edge, above all because I have to keep quiet and show I'm strong to give everyone else courage . . ."

"Surveillance is tighter than ever, I can't take a step without 'guardian angels' at my heels. What a lovely feeling! 'A hell of a life!' [This phrase was in English although the rest of the letter was in Dutch.] How will it all end? . . . You can't imagine what an inferno it is here, especially after the trial of the cardinal" (presumably a reference to Mindszenty, who had been tried earlier that month).

The regime bullied the Protestant and Catholic Churches but blandished the Orthodox Church, which had the allegiance of over 90 percent of the population. The Communists described it as the traditional Church of Bulgaria: in other words, they wanted its support and were prepared to give it financial and other help. The Orthodox accepted the new religious law. But Bossilkov refused to do so even though he predicted that would mean "a cage" (prison) for him.

In 1949 the Vatican's representative in Bulgaria was expelled because "the Vatican is an implacable enemy of the Soviet Union, of Peoples' Democracies (Communist regimes), and of Communism and serves dark forces (the United States) which are preparing a new world war." Catholic hospitals, clinic, and orphanages were closed and the nuns who served them dispersed. Even priests' homes were seized. The Catholic publishing house and weekly newspaper were suppressed. Foreign missionaries were expelled.

Having rid itself of possible troublesome witnesses such as the Vatican's representative and foreign missionaries, in 1950 the regime intensified its anti-Catholic campaigns. First it arrested a Capuchin father who had edited the suppressed weekly, then a second Capuchin, as if the threat of arrests might induce other priests and bishops to be more accommodating.

After two years of relentless interrogations, brutal treatment, and debilitating drugs, the first Capuchin was brought to a public show trial for anti-Communist activity and spying. Although emaciated, the aged priest did not indulge in self-accusations, as the Communists had hoped, but instead defended himself before receiving a fourteen-year sentence. After this defiance, the trial of his confrere was held in secret, even though that vitiated its aim of discrediting the Catholic Church.

The Stalinists of the Bulgarian Communist Party decided to step up the offensive. At dawn on July 16, 1952, police raids were made: Bishop Bossilkov, twenty-seven priests, some religious and laity, including ten Orthodox who allegedly collaborated with the Catholics, were arrested.

The trial did not take place until the end of September. During it, Bossilkov was allowed to meet some relatives and told them, "They've inflicted satanic tortures." A shirt he wore at the trial, which was later returned to relatives, was bloodstained. A relative recounted that, while awaiting trial, Bishop Bossilkov had heard the screams of the superior of the Bulgarian Franciscans from a nearby cell. When the Franciscan died under torture, the guards had invited Bossilkov to look at what awaited him, but he had refused.

On a table in the courtroom in Sofia was the evidence against the accused: an old machine gun, two pistols, some hand grenades, and empty cartridges taken from a Catholic college's exhibition on a Bulgarian World War I victory. From the same college came a typewriter and a radio allegedly used to send secret messages abroad. Bishop Bossilkov was accused of using a Marian Association to oppose the regime.

Many of the arrested had signed confessions but in court denied them and defended themselves. A Communist who was present has testified to Bossilkov's courageous defense, which embarrassed the judges. Some senior officials of the Ministry for Religion took the risk of speaking in his defense. But one of the accused renounced the pope, then attributed to himself and his bishop, Ivan Romanoff, even more than the state charged. (Bishop Romanoff, who was seventy-three and had a weak heart, was arrested immediately, tried in secret, and condemned to twenty years of forced labor; he died in prison the following year.)

On October 3 Bossilkov and three priests were ordered to be shot; the other priests and laity, including the Orthodox, received prison sentences, and their possessions were confiscated. On October 5, the Vatican daily *L'Osservatore Romano* described the trial as "an alibi for a planned murder." On November 11, Bossilkov was shot.

After Bossilkov's sentence, his relatives had visited him and promised to seek stay of execution. But Bossilkov, who had chains on his leg and arm, told them not to worry as he "felt the Lord would give him the strength to welcome death." He asked for food, money, and blankets as he was sleeping on cement. To another visitor, he said he felt "overwhelmed by God's grace," adding, "I will die willingly for the Faith."

Bulgarian Communist authorities opposed Bossilkov's beatification process, which had to begin from an Italian diocese. This pressure induced Cardinal Pietro Palazzini, head of the Vatican Congregation for the Causes of Saints, to announce that the process had been postponed, but he did not say whether it was for years, months, or minutes. In fact, in 1994 the beatification of Bossilkov was approved, but the ceremony may not take place until a Bulgarian government is prepared to admit the crime perpetrated by the earlier regime.

Bossilkov's story captures the horrific atmosphere of the Stalinist era, in which many other bishops, priests, members of religious orders, and laity were harshly persecuted. But failing to crush religion, Communist regimes moved at diverse speeds and with some switchbacks to gradual de facto acceptance of it, as if it were a vice such as tobacco smoking that had to be controlled. Christians' right to worship was recognized, but only atheism had a right to proselytize. Christians were hedged about with constraints, education was slanted against them, and their career possibilities were nil. They were excluded from the Party and therefore from most public life. This effectively applied the principle of natural selection in the spiritual sphere, as it discouraged the weak-spirited but did not daunt the zealous.

———

Stalin's deportations led, ironically, to a proliferation of Catholic communities beyond the Urals, bringing them to lands where, it has been said, "no one would ever go voluntarily." He was following the precedent of the czars, who had considered Siberia a huge prison for political exiles. Catholicism took root there when 20,000 Polish families were deported after the 1830 Polish revolt against Russian suzerainty. Under Stalin, more than two million Poles were deported from occupied Poland and Soviet zones near the Polish border.

The other major group in the region were Germans. Peter the Great had invited German artisans to Russia, but it was a German princess who, a year after she became Empress Catherine in 1762, opened the doors to German peasants. They settled mainly in the Volga region with a right to retain their nationality and religion. However, as the Nazi army advanced during World War II, Stalin deported the Volga Germans, who numbered more than 1.5 million, beyond the Urals, not even sparing the many who were serving in the Red Army. A large proportion were Catholic, and in prohibitive circumstances they preserved their religion as essential to their cultural identity.

There were many Catholics also among the Ukrainian, Lithuanian, and other deportees. There were also priests, and after they died others arrived. State supervision of priests working in Asia was less rigorous than in European Soviet republics. Moreover, in a state where the cross was often represented rising above the sickle moon of Islam, some officials may not have been unhappy to have even Catholic priests in largely Muslim regions. (In Kazakhstan, the number of Kazakhs, who are Muslims, exceeded that of Russians for the first time in the 1980s.)

Józef Świdnicki is a man who studied theology perched between heaven and earth; each day for a year he sat in a crane on a deserted construction site in Riga, Latvia, rounding out his seminary studies. Born on Christmas Day 1936 in Sherminka, between Kiev and Odessa, he studied construction engineering at Kiev University but abandoned his course to enter the Riga seminary, which served all of the Soviet Union except Lithuania and had as many as twelve students in each small bedroom.

The Soviet authorities, however, rejected Józef's request to enter the seminary, so he worked six months for the railways and then seven years as a crane driver at the port of Riga. Each year he applied unsuccessfully for the seminary, but nevertheless continued his studies. In 1966 he lived illegally in the seminary for two months and passed its examinations. He then enrolled at the Riga campus of Leningrad University to complete his construction-engineering course but six months before the final examinations, for no given reason, was expelled. The local bishop sent Józef to a Lithuanian bishop, Vincentas Sladkevičius (later made a cardinal), who ordained him.

For the next four years Józef worked as a crane driver on a building site, taking alternate weeks off because he did two shifts at a time. Russian hippies, curious about religion and coming mainly from professional families, approached him after they had found Orthodox priests unsympathetic; eventually he baptized thirty of them. In his free weeks he ministered to Catholics in Belarus and Ukraine. When the builders were sent to a different site, the cranes and other equipment remained idle for a year. This provided a heaven-sent opportunity for Józef to complete his theological studies: God rules straight with idle cranes.

In 1974, some Catholics came from Zytomyr, Ukraine, to Riga and stayed three days, begging the bishop for a priest. Józef went to minister in Zytomyr, but a year later a K.G.B. agent complained that it would take a decade to undo what Józef had done. Although ordered to leave, Józef managed to remain another six months as a night watchman while continuing his ministry.

Antonyi Giey, a Belarusan who was working as a stoker in a Riga museum while completing his seminary studies (by 1993 he was a parish priest in Moscow), advised Józef to go to Kazakhstan, where Giey had grown up because his parents had been deported there. Józef went illegally, and then went even further to Tajikistan on the Afghan border, a region which is largely desert and mountains, the Pamirs, which rise over 21,000 feet. The weather can be scorching by day and cold that same night. It is one of five republics, formerly known as West Turkistan, which have a total of 45 million inhabitants, 80 percent of whom are Sunni Muslims. When Józef arrived in the capital, Dushanbe, it had 500,000 inhabitants. Set in a green valley, it consisted largely of prefabricated houses and office blocks from the Stalin era.

In Dushanbe the Catholics, mainly of German origin, had for many years met in the cemetery to say the rosary but in the mid 1970s received permission to use a house as a church. Groups of twenty or more believers could apply for registration, which enabled them to worship in public and employ a minister of religion. Originally the house-church held only fifty persons but the parishioners gradually extended it by working at night and camouflaging the new sections each dawn. Józef not only served as priest for this church but also found use for his engineering skills, building two churches and a chapel for six new communities that obtained state registration. He also organized five youth groups before the K.G.B. forced him to move on once more.

Józef transferred to Novosibirsk in Siberia and took responsibility for the faithful in Tomsk and Tseljabinsk. During the next five years he established communities there which obtained state registration; he bought houses to serve as chapels and in Novosibirsk built a house in which two hundred people could attend Mass.

Early on December 19, 1984, police knocked at his door. They accused him of being an extremist and charged him with subversion. On searching his apartment, they found a book on Our Lady of Fatima with a prayer for the conversion of Russia. That evening a judge told him the attempt at conversion was an insult: "What do you want to convert us to? Freedom, happiness?" Józef was sentenced for "plotting against authorities, organizing youth groups in secret, and claiming that Catholics are persecuted." Although the judge said that Józef deserved eight years' imprisonment, he sentenced the priest to three in a labor camp.

Józef spent the first five months with thirty-five other people in a room of about twenty square yards. Their work consisted of making 60 wooden chests each eight hours, which meant driving a total of 3,000 nails daily. After three months, because Józef was one of the fastest workers, his conditions were improved. By the time he was released in 1987, he had completed apprenticeships in five trades. He had served only two years and four months but fortunately was the last on a list of 150 priests to be freed under the *perestroika* policy: while Józef was driving nails, Mikhail Gorbachev had come to power.

On his return to Novosibirsk, Józef found the atmosphere had improved: a church he had planned had been built, and his place as pastor had been taken by a young Lithuanian Franciscan. One thing remained unchanged however: the K.G.B. still had his number. He was told to leave. He went first to Dushanbe, then headed for Fergana in Uzbekistan. Many of its

Catholics, mostly of German origin, subsequently fled because of conflicts between the major ethnic groups, the Uzbeks and Turkmens. Józef ministered to various small Catholic communities of diverse ethnic origin (Tartar, Russian, and Dutch, as well as Polish, Ukrainian, German, and Lithuanian).

If the hedgehog knows one thing and the fox many, Józef was a fox, for he seemed to take Soviet Asia as his parish. Albinas Dumbliauskas, on the other hand, was a hedgehog: although he was not allowed to stay put, he was singleminded and at times criticized Józef for being a gadfly.

Beefy, blue-eyed, large-featured, Albinas had the solid serenity of a family doctor, although in his last years he became prickly. In his native Lithuania, Communist authorities, complaining that this Jesuit attracted too many young people, prohibited him from ministering. A priest friend who worked in secret in Siberia had run into similar difficulties with officials: he had been despatched home to Lithuania when found conducting a funeral service near Irkutsk. He spoke to Albinas about the needs of Catholics in Siberia. After the ban on his priestly activity in Lithuania, Albinas worked as an ambulance driver, arranging his shifts so that every two months he had two weeks off. During these free weeks, Albinas drove over 3,000 miles to Siberia: he would leave on Wednesday and by Sunday night was celebrating Mass in the house of a Catholic family or in the woods. He took vestments and hosts with him, and the faithful supplied wine.

After six years of this, in 1968 Bishop Juozapas Labukas summoned Albinas to say that Catholics from Kustanay in Kazakhstan had requested a priest. State officials in Moscow, Labukas added, delayed responding to requests for a permit, but if Albinas wanted to work clandestinely in Kustanay he would have the bishop's blessing.

To reach Kazakhstan, head southeast from Moscow and turn left at the Caspian Sea. It runs all the way, beneath Siberia, to

Mongolia. As large as Western Europe, it is scarcely populated. Going to Kazakhstan, it has been said, is a one-way ticket to hell: in winter breath freezes on beards, the summers are torrid. Albinas could not wait to get there.

In Kustanay, he built a church and organized the laity, but eventually the mayor summoned him to say he had decided to close the church. "We thought only old women would go there," he told Albinas, "but you're filling it with youth." He advised Albinas to return to Lithuania, as the unemployed were considered parasites. Instead Albinas hid until a friend told him that the Kustanay hospital needed an ambulance driver. He resumed his former occupation for seven years, learning also to assist doctors and saying Mass most Sunday nights in the woods.

Albinas heard that 15,000 Catholics in the coal-mining town of Karaganda (Black City) wanted a priest. He went there as often as possible. The Catholics were the survivors and descendants of Germans who had been deported from the Volga region during the war. As Soviet police had told them they would make a brief train journey, they carried few things with them when they left. The journey took two months because the railway was still being laid down. There were many deaths in the overcrowded carriages: the corpses were buried beside the tracks, but there was no wood to make crosses. Finally the deportees reached their destination, a steppe distant from the coal mines where they were to slave. As there was no accommodation, with their own hands they had to dig trenches in the frozen soil. Some lived on that site for twenty years.

By the mid 1970s the situation had changed: the Soviet Union was trying desperately to increase coal production. Authorities in Karaganda decided to placate the Germans by approving construction of a church, with Albinas as its priest. A priest had come with the deportees but had been shot shortly after arrival and had not been replaced. Albinas agreed but, loath to have his work truncated again as in Kustanay, said he first wanted authorization from Moscow. This arrived in January 1977, after a mere ten months, which was unusually swift for Soviet bureaucracy. That same day the parishioners set to work on the church, which was completed by March 19, the feast of St. Joseph, whose name it took. Albinas was pensioned off as an ambulance driver and, at fifty-two, again became a priest in the light of day. Six years later, after guiding their preliminary studies, he was able to send six local youths to the Riga seminary. It was a late harvest for a tenacious priest. Albinas died in Karaganda in 1991 without returning home.

One of the youths Albinas prepared for the priesthood was Aleksandr Kahn. His parents were deported during the war—his father from Moscow, his mother from Ukraine—because they were ethnically German. They met in Gavanj gulag near Vladivostok, where Aleksandr's father was sentenced to ten years' imprisonment for attempting to kill a sadistic camp guard. Aleksandr's mother waited the ten years, they married and were allowed to go to Kazakhstan where, like many other deportees, they searched for relatives.

In seven years, they had four sons and three daughters (Aleksandr was next to last), then separated. The maternal grandmother, Serafine, came to live with the family so that the mother could work in a silo. They were living in Tobol, a town built around a railway station, whose 10,000 inhabitants were of many nationalities and faiths: 40 percent Orthodox, 20 percent Muslim, with minorities of Catholics, Lutherans, and other Christians. In the evening Christians met freely in each others' homes to pray because there were no churches. In Aleksandr's house there were many images of the Madonna and saints, but atheistic teachers came on friendly visits, as did Muslims. The grandmother, Serafine, baptized and officiated at marriages provisionally until a roving clandestine priest arrived. Aleksandr first saw a priest, a visiting Ukrainian Franciscan, when he was thirteen. Perhaps some of Aleksandr's atheistic schooling had stuck—he took an instant dislike to the priest and refused to return home while the Franciscan was present.

In 1978, when the death of a relative made an apartment available, the family moved to Karaganda. There Aleksandr met an old bishop exiled from Ukraine, Aleksandr Khira, who all in one day heard his confession, gave him his first communion, and confirmed him. He then invited Aleksandr for a meal. Khira's warmth dissolved Aleksandr's distrust of priests.

On completing secondary school, Aleksandr became a truck driver at a venereal disease hospital for a year. He then did two years of military service in the place where his mother, while in a gulag, had worked on construction of a Siberian railway. He decided to become a priest and, on return to Karaganda, lived with Albinas Dumbliauskas, who prepared him for the Riga seminary and the Jesuit order. The K.G.B. sought Aleksandr's collaboration, asking him to inform them of any "enemies of the fatherland" in the seminary. On Albinas's advice, Aleksandr expressed good will but refused to sign anything—his ultimate deterrent was to point out that he could always become a priest clandestinely. Aleksandr was admitted to the Riga seminary and, after working as a priest in Kazakhstan, began studying canon law at the Gregorian University in Rome.

Albinas also influenced the priestly vocations of the six Messmer brothers of a Volga German family living in Kazakhstan. In 1973 one of them, Hieronimus, decided to become a priest, but the Council for Religious Affairs would not let him enter the Riga seminary. Instead he began military service at Kurgan-Tyube near the Afghanistan frontier, where he met the man who had studied theology halfway to heaven in a crane in Riga, Józef Świdnicki. Józef's advice to Hieronimus was to seek work locally after completing his military service. Hieronimus found factory work until allowed to enter Riga seminary. In 1986, on completion of his studies, Messmer became parish priest of Dushanbe, where there had been several unofficial successors to Józef Świdnicki. Almost two decades after the end of the Vatican Council, one of them had introduced its new liturgical practices. Without any outside donations, the Catholic community of Dushanbe in 1986 built a new central-city church with gleaming white walls and the only working organ in Tajikistan, brought there from an Armenian Catholic cemetery chapel in Moldova where it had fallen into disuse.

Hieronimus had a hectic schedule, as he was responsible also for two other communities near the Afghanistan border—by 1993 the church of one of these communities closed because its members had left for Germany or Russia. From the beginning of the 1990s, much of the Central Asia region has been afflicted by ethnic strife and has felt the influence of Iranian Muslim fundamentalists. In 1991 the Russian military had helped Communists return to power in Tajikistan, but 20,000 had died in the struggle and guerilla fighting continued. Ceremonies in the church in central Dushanbe are sometimes disturbed by the noise of tanks deployed against conflicting groups. Half the congregation has left, some because of the turmoil, and others because Europeans are resented. But Hieronimus said he would not leave while needed.

In 1989 Hieronimus's elder brother, Nikolaus, became the parish priest in Frunze (now Bishkek), a city of 600,000 inhabitants and the capital of the neighboring republic of Kirghizstan. The parishioners had to wait five years while he completed his seminary studies before he could replace his predecessor, another Volga-German priest.

A third Messmer, Otto, is parish priest in Akmola, a city of 300,000 in Kazakhstan, most of whose Catholics are ethnically

Poles or Ukrainians. They did not see a priest for years until one arrived in 1956 and, for a week, in secret celebrated baptisms, marriages, and other sacraments before moving on into the pale white yonder. It was a decade before Catholics there saw another priest: several who tried to reach them had been arrested. For years Otto Messmer used a house outside the town as a church but, in 1993, received a central site on which to build one. As Kazakhstan is potentially rich, those of Polish or Ukrainian origin have not left in such proportions as from other former Soviet Asian republics where, paradoxically, freedom for Catholics to exercise their faith was followed by the departure of many of them.

———

Catholics in Soviet Asia were largely concerned with preserving their religious, ethnic, and cultural identity in a hostile environment. Many Orthodox in Russia were concerned rather with witnessing to their faith in the face both of an atheistic state and of what they claimed was a servile Church hierarchy.

Russian Orthodoxy had suffered atrociously under a Communist regime which, when it found it could not destroy the Church altogether, decided to domesticate it. The Orthodox claim that 140,000 priests, monks, and nuns were executed in the 1920s and 1930s while 45,000 churches were closed or destroyed. In 1929 laws were introduced which proclaimed freedom of worship but prevented the Church from any public activities, religious, social, or cultural. At the same time, the atheistic League of the Godless was allowed to attack the Church and Christians. Church buildings were turned into stables and storehouses, seminaries and monasteries were closed, and priests were attacked as "ideological kulaks" (the peasant proprietors destroyed during the agrarian collectivization program).

Stalinist purges seemed about to crush the Orthodox Church, when the dictator was forced to seek its support against Nazi invaders. Persecution was violent again in the 1960s because, although Nikita Khrushchev was comparatively liberal in some respects, he was aggressively antireligious. (The contrast in Khrushchev's personality is captured in the statue by Edward Neizvestnyi above Khrushchev's tomb at the cemetery of the Novodevichy Monastery in Moscow: one side of his body is white, the other black.) The state controlled all aspects of Christian life from baptism (which had to be registered) to seminary entrance. Not content to break the Church's body, the Party wanted to seduce its soul. All priests were asked to become informers. The backs of many bishops were broken, but some of them tested the limits of the system and strengthened the Church, for instance by improving seminary training. One, Bishop Yermogen, used his legal training to defend Orthodoxy in his diocese of Kaluga near the Urals. Even during Khrushchev's antireligious campaign, Yermogen prevented the closure of any of his diocese's churches. In 1970 he died in exile.

Other Orthodox took the risk of acting on their convictions. The portly Aleksandr Men, who was part Jew, had trained as a biologist but converted to Christianity along with his mother. He became a priest and one of Russia's most influential preachers, and brought many scientists, artists, and young people to Orthodoxy. In a Moscow street on September 9, 1990, a man wielding an axe bludgeoned him to death. In 1994 it was announced that a local resident, whose name was not disclosed, had confessed to the killing.

Even though his mother was a devout Orthodox, Gleb Jakunin was involved with yoga and theosophy while studying biology. Partly through the influence of Aleksandr Men, he became a convinced Christian and, at the age of twenty-seven, a priest. In 1965 he wrote an open letter to the Patriarch of Moscow in which he denounced the Church's subservience to power and its "pernicious silence." It was the first of a series of public denunciations which brought him Church and state censure, although he did have support from Bishop Yermogen. Despairing of any similar initiative by the hierarchy, in 1976 Jakunin and others founded the Central Committee for the Defense of Believers' Rights in the USSR. Four years later he was sentenced for anti-Soviet propaganda to five years of imprisonment and five years of exile. The slight, red-haired priest's habitual tension seemed to disappear when sentenced, for he said, "I am pleased the Lord has sent me this cross, which I accept with joy."

Aleksandr Ogorodnikov found his interest in Christianity awakened when he saw Pier Paolo Pasolini's film *The Gospel according to St. Matthew.* This interest, he claims, brought his expulsion from the Moscow Film Institute.

"My friends and I grew up in atheistic families," Ogorodnikov has explained. "Each of us made a complicated, sometimes agonizing spiritual search. We started from Marxism, experienced nihilism and the total rejection of all ideology, were attracted to the 'hippie' lifestyle, but finally came to the Church."

In 1974 in Moscow, twenty-two-year-old Ogorodnikov founded a study circle, the Christian Seminar, which aimed to give its members a theological education, to dialogue with other Christian denominations, and to take Christianity beyond the narrow confines permitted by the state, promoting "liberation of the Russian Church from the offensive yoke of state patronage." Although one of the founders affirmed that social action was the way to deepen spiritual life, the group's activities were confined to organizing talks, holding discussions, and publishing one issue of a clandestine journal.

Harassment of its members began in 1976. Ogorodnikov lost his job and had to leave the capital. In 1979 he received a year's sentence for "parasitism" (the crime of being wilfully unemployed; in fact, when arrested, Ogorodnikov was on his way to start a new job) and, before release, received an additional six-year sentence to a strict-regime labor camp to be followed by five years in exile. In 1986, for violating camp regulations, he was sentenced to a further three years. He was becoming a permanent resident of the Gulag Archipelago, where, as he wrote, "any manifestation of such Christian impulses as mercy, compassion, defense of the persecuted, and love" was forbidden.

Ogorodnikov spent a total of 411 days in solitary confinement, three spells in an internal camp prison, and 659 non-consecutive days on a partial hunger strike to support his demand for a Bible, a prayer book, and a crucifix. He was given five days in solitary confinement for writing out the fiftieth psalm: "Let our God come, and be silent no more . . . You are leaving God out of account, take care." When he finished the hunger strike, he had to assemble electrical appliances but, as he could not fulfill the quotas, was given a low-calorie diet, only one-third of the United Nations sustenance level, which did not enable him to recover his strength. In April 1984, when he wrote in his diary that he was just "skin and bones," he fainted several times. Tranquilizers were administered, which brought him close to nervous collapse; delirious and in solitary confinement, he slashed his wrists but was saved. Among the charges against Ogorodnikov in his 1986 trial were that he said morning prayers and influenced other inmates to do likewise.

"At the root of the camp regime," Ogorodnikov later wrote, "lies an immoral and insatiable desire for power per se. Camp discipline embodies the ideologues' secret intent to create a finished design for the Soviet society of tomorrow. It decrees uniformity in clothing, appearance, behavior, and ways of thinking as an interim measure until full control over these areas can be achieved . . . The crippling work load, the food, the sleep routine, the monotony, and inescapable predetermination of every action are all designed to bring you down from your rightful status as one made in the image and likeness of God to a dull, undiscriminating, slavish, animal-like condition, so that you are capable only of grabbing at any slight chance of filling your clamoring belly . . . The main objects of the regime's hatred are God, the spirit, the word, and man's need to live in a cultural context."

Gulags were an extreme form of a system which had convinced Ogorodnikov and his friends that there was a desperate need for spiritual and social renewal. His right-hand man in the Christian Seminar was Vladimir Poresch, who kept a baby buggy outside his two-bedroom Leningrad apartment because inside there was no room for it. In 1989 he was living there with his wife, their four children, who ranged from three months to ten years, his mother-in-law, and his sister-in-law. Vladimir worked as a stoker four days a week and painted houses as a second job. A specialist in Romance philology, he had been a researcher in French literature at the Library of the Academy of Science until his family outgrew his monthly 120 rubles ($40) salary. As a stoker he earned 150 rubles and, in a good month, spare-time house painting brought him considerably more. He paid 25 rubles for rent; two pounds of meat cost three rubles. He could afford a roomier apartment but none was available.

Tatiana Shipkova, who later joined the Christian Seminar, recalled rangy, big-handed Poresch joining her French class at the Smolensk Pedagogical Institute in 1966: aged seventeen, from an atheistic household, he thought that religion had developed from fear of the forces of nature. When he continued his studies at Leningrad University, he wrote to Tatiana, nineteen years his senior, about his solitude and despair: "all spiritual life is senseless . . . it is senseless to keep searching but I shall go on . . ." Later he felt tempted to suicide, but in 1973 this urge was transformed by his reading Christian authors such as Fyodor Dostoyevsky and by meeting "Sasha"

Ogorodnikov. "We've decided to create a culture within a culture," he told Tatiana. (Because she talked about first-century Christianity in her ancient culture classes and even told the students, to their surprise, that Christianity was still alive, Tatiana was forced out of her teaching post, while her son and two other relatives were expelled from the Institute.)

On October 20, 1974, Vladimir was baptized. From Leningrad he began to collaborate with the Christian Seminar in Moscow. In July 1976, he was shadowed and roughed up by K.G.B. agents when bringing documents to Ogorodnikov. A K.G.B. agent had spotted him on arrival at a Moscow subway station, and as Vladimir tried to throw off his "tail" the number of agents constantly increased. On August 1, 1979, he was sentenced for producing the only issue of the Christian Seminar's journal, but he survived imprisonment with his faith intact.

There were other Christian study groups. One was organized in Leningrad by Sergei Grib, an astrophysicist who was subject to K.G.B. harassment when his ecumenical contacts were discovered; this group met in the apartment of Elena Kazimirtchak-Polonskaya.

Elena was a Russian who was born on her family's estate in West Ukraine in 1908. After graduating in astronomy from Lviv University, she married a Pole who was the estate manager and had a son by him. When her husband was taken by the Nazis, she sought him in the nearest concentration camp. "You can go in," a German officer had told her, "but you can't come out." A day's search convinced Elena that her husband was not there, and she did manage to leave.

She was seeking him in Warsaw at the time the Soviet army waited across the Vistula River while German troops destroyed the inner city and much of its population. German soldiers stopped Elena and were on the point of shooting her but desisted when she told them that their mothers might eventually face the same threat from Soviet troops.

Elena did not find her husband in Warsaw either, but she eventually heard that he had married again. Bringing her son and many Bibles with her, she went to Kherson in the Soviet Union, where she lectured in mathematics at the Pedagogical Institute. Arrested for propagating Christianity, she obtained release by convincing the prison director that Christianity provided socially useful moral guidance. She was aided also by her earlier newspaper articles advocating Russian-Ukrainian friendship.

In prison her second doctoral thesis, necessary to obtain promotion from lecturer to professor, was stolen by an inmate who was leaving; he passed it off as his own but was later exposed. After writing another thesis, Elena, who specialized in the study of comets, became a professor at the Leningrad Institute of Theoretical Astronomy.

When Elena's son died of scarlet fever, to her great regret she was not allowed to give him a religious funeral.

Convinced that there was no contradiction between faith and science or between Eastern and Western spirituality, she was an enthusiastic member of the study circle which explored what was involved in sainthood, whether Russian—as exemplified by figures like Aleksandr Nevsky and Sergei of Radonez—or Western—as seen in figures like Francis of Assisi and Therese of Lisieux. The study circle members also analyzed what news they had of Christian activities worldwide.

Shortly before her death at the age of eighty-four in 1992, Elena Kazimirtchak-Polonskaya became an Orthodox nun but continued her computer-based study of comets. She began also to lecture at the St. Petersburg Theological Academy on figures such as the theologian Sergei Bulgakov.

A generation of dedicated Orthodox who had been raised in atheistic households had found they needed something more. Mostly university graduates, they undermined the stereotype that the Russian Orthodox Church consisted of kerchiefed grandmothers. Their links were with the *samizdat* (underground publications) counterculture rather than with the official Church.

Another Elena, strong-faced with high cheek bones and curly brown hair, is one of these new-breed Christians. Her mother is a militant atheist called Lenina (after Lenin) who, Elena said drily, "believes in the devil but not in God." Her father is an Iranian lecturer in history at Moscow university. Elena felt that everyone in Russia lived in fear and that there was no way of breaking out of it. But, on a trip to Lithuania, she sensed that the Catholics she saw at Mass had the truth she lacked. On her return to Moscow she sometimes heard prayers in Lithuanian on Vatican Radio and, although she did not know the language, wanted to be able to pray with similar conviction. She married and had a daughter Catherine, but the marriage broke up.

A decade after her visit to Lithuania she became a Catholic and married Andrei Bessmertny, a strapping fellow with the self-confidence of one who has grown up conscious of being part of an elite and bearing a name of good omen—Bessmertny means "immortal." His grandparents had been well-to-do St. Petersburg Orthodox. One of them was killed by a Bolshevik revolutionary, but Andrei's father became a Communist and a successful documentary film-maker. Professionally Andrei followed his father, working as a researcher at the Moscow Film Institute.

Until he was ten, Andrei presumed that Communism was on the way to rightful world domination. However, although God was rarely mentioned in his home, his imagination was stimulated by churches and, later, by the attention to religion of writers such as Aleksandr Pushkin, Nikolai Gogol, Leo Tolstoy, Robert Louis Stevenson, Charles Dickens, and Mark Twain. He found a New Testament which was lent to him boring, but he was curious enough to attend a church one Easter. Because of this, Komsomol (Communist Youth League) members tried to have him excluded from a Languages Institute. Andrei thwarted them by pulling political strings, which he described wryly as an example of "corruption in the Party." But the episode made him wonder why he could not freely go to church.

"I wanted to ask the lecturers on Marxism and Leninism at the Languages Institute if they were kidding," Andrei recalled when interviewed in his roomy apartment near the Moscow River. "It was the greyest, most uninteresting philosophy I had ever heard."

It certainly could not compare with Dickens or Tolstoy, and even the New Testament had now begun to arouse his interest. In 1974 Andrei was baptized. "I found everything in literature, art, and cinema became clearer after baptism," he said. "I read the Gospels with empathy and saw things more deeply. I realized that Christ had been born for me, that he suffered for me—and all K.G.B. members too."

Educating children as Christians was difficult when schools taught that Jesus Christ was a fiction. To offset this influence on Elena's daughter Catherine and others, Andrei organized a Sunday school for both children and adults. This brought a visit from K.G.B. agents who were startled to find, in the Bessmertny living room, a photograph of John Paul II. Asked for an explanation, Andrei said that the Orthodox and Catholic Churches were really one. He spoke well of the pope.

"Do you know who's behind him?"

"I take it God is."

"No," said the K.G.B. man, letting Andrei in on the secret. "It's the C.I.A."

Andrei was accused of organizing a Sunday school and of having written an anonymous article on Soviet Christians for a Russian emigrants' magazine in Paris. Both charges were true, but Andrei's trial did not take place, because of more liberal policies introduced by Mikhail Gorbachev.

Elena explained that Christian beliefs supply a spiritual and moral framework otherwise missing. "At school Stalin was our hero, but then his photograph was ripped from our schoolbooks. We were taught Brezhnev was a great man but then he was blamed for 'stagnation.' There have been so many changes in so many spheres that, unless they're Christian, children don't believe anything. They feel all is permitted because all norms are temporary."

Chapter 4

Heeding a Quiet Voice

Often the essence of liberty is revealed only through
oppression and imprisonment; but at what a price!

Doina Cornea

As well as steadfast Catholics in Siberia and atheistically
educated European Russians who discovered Christianity,
certain individuals in other countries, as will be evident
from the following accounts, refused to compromise.

——

Her beatific smile is the first thing one notices about Nijolė
Sadūnaitė: as she listens to others, it sometimes lights up
her face as if she is heeding instead an inner voice. The
second thing one notices is her buoyancy. These qualities
frustrated her interrogators. When the secret police
arrested Nijolė, whom they called "the most dangerous
person in Lithuania," she joked with them, offered to pray
for them, and was indifferent to their threats. She had seen
her father being interrogated by Soviet officials, and her
grandparents had been deported to Siberia. As many other
Lithuanians, her family had a tradition of suffering under
the Russians.

Her father was a teacher of agricultural science who had
traveled in Europe and in Africa. Shortly after Nijolė's birth
in 1939, he had to flee from possible deportation to Siberia

with her, his son Jonas, and his wife, who suffered from bone tuberculosis. A seminary employed him as a teacher so that the family would find refuge; later he became a consultant on a model farm. The family lived in the woods nearby, but whenever anyone unfamiliar approached they hid amid the crops.

Because they refused to join the Communist Youth League, Nijolė and Jonas were expelled from secondary school but were readmitted after a few weeks—perhaps because Nijolė excelled in sports such as volleyball, basketball, and ping-pong. She intended to become a physical education teacher but desisted because a profession of Marxist atheism was required. Instead she joined a clandestine community of nuns. A Communist youth paper complained that a promising sportswoman had been lost.

As a nun (although without a habit) Nijolė worked in a hospital near the capital, Vilnius, as this enabled her to obtain an apartment, where she lived with her sick and by now widowed mother. In 1963 they managed to bring Nijolė's widowed grandmother Carolina back from Siberia.

Subsequently Nijolė worked as a typist, factory worker, then as a clerk in the statistics department of Vilnius University. In 1970 Nijolė contacted a lawyer to defend a priest on trial for the crime of teaching catechism. Because of this, she was forced to resign from her job at the university. She qualified as a nurse and worked with abandoned children, but the K.G.B. was on her track because anyone who organized the defense of a "criminal" was suspect.

Some Lithuanian Catholics believed they should work quietly within the little space the Communists conceded but others wanted, nonviolently, to challenge the regime. In 1972 the latter founded *The Chronicle of the Catholic Church in Lithuania,* which recorded violations of human and religious rights. Material was gathered from all over Lithuania and then typed, with seven carbon copies at a time, usually by nuns working almost nonstop near a wood fire where, if raided, they could burn everything. Copies were smuggled out of Lithuania, then translated and published abroad, to attract international attention. Sometimes copies were hidden in religious statues which were carried away by visiting tourists; at other times they were taken by a priest or nun who usually set out on a pastoral task to confound "minders," then took a train to Moscow, where a copy was given to a contact such as a Russian dissident or a Westerner who could get it out of the Soviet Union.

Although even some sacristies were bugged, the K.G.B. did not identify the editorial staff in the seventeen years from 1972 to 1989, during which eighty-three issues appeared, some of them over a hundred pages long. Only one typed *Chronicle* was not published. As Nijolė was typing it, the K.G.B. entered her apartment. She dived in a closet with it and, before the K.G.B. found her, shredded it. On leaving the closet, she said she had to use the lavatory, where she flushed away the shredded typescript. But she was arrested for typing the *Chronicle.*

"The *Chronicle* reflects like a mirror atheists' crimes against believers," Nijolė said in court. "Immorality is frightened to see its repugnant aspect mirrored, so you hate those who try to snatch from your face the mask of lies and hypocrisy. But this does not disqualify the mirror! Thieves steal money, but you rob what is most precious: people's fidelity to their beliefs and their possibility of transmitting this treasure to their children . . . You want to make people your spiritual slaves. Thank God not all have submitted. It is everyone's sacred duty to struggle for human rights."

When interviewed, she recalled that as she spoke the public prosecutor and the judge kept their eyes lowered as if they were being sentenced. "Poor things," she commented, "they must have known they were committing a crime."

Nijolė was sentenced to three years of hard labor followed by three years in Siberia. Although not tortured or beaten, she discovered the Soviet use of suffocatingly hot and freezingly cold cells to break prisoners' resistance. "My faith saved me," she said. "I learned in prison that not even the K.G.B. can destroy what's best in human nature."

In 1980, she returned to Lithuania and two years later foiled another arrest attempt while on her way to see her brother, Jonas, who had been sentenced to thirteen months in a psychiatric hospital. After her escape, she lived in hiding and used various disguises while continuing to work for the *Chronicle.* She would take copies by train to Moscow, where sympathizers managed to send them to the West. In 1987 she was again arrested and interrogated. She was advised to leave Lithuania but responded that she preferred to go to prison— and to Paradise—with her interrogators. At a certain moment, all but one of the interrogators left the underground interrogation room. The remaining officer asked if she weren't afraid she might finish, as had some troublesome priests, under a car. "It doesn't matter where or how I die," she answered, "as long as I keep love for all people in my heart."

Given a meal, she was then told her food contained a drug which would incapacitate her will without reducing her lucidity. She was asked the name of the person in Moscow to whom she had given the *Chronicle* for despatch abroad. Fortunately she knew only the person's Christian name, which was useless to the interrogators.

Nijolė was released but constantly shadowed. Once she gave the agent following her the slip. When he caught up, she was in a telephone booth and smiled radiantly. He swore; she asked if a law against smiling had been introduced. In 1988, as she walked near the church of St. Anne in Vilnius, a car drew up and three men jumped out. One punched her in the solar plexus, the others grabbed her; but passers-by came to her help, and the three attackers drove off. In July 1990 she was rehabilitated despite all her "crimes" in favor of religious liberty. Nijolė had become a symbol of Lithuania's religiously-inspired resistance, which steadfastly refused to respond violently to violence.

"My most significant formative experience," said Sigitas Tamkevičius, interviewed in Kaunas, "was when the Communists prohibited me from functioning as a priest. I worked for a year in a factory, then drained swamps, digging channels but also conducting spiritual retreats. I found how to work clandestinely with youth and also how to prepare underground publications."

In other words, the Communists forced Tamkevičius to break the clerical mold and be inventive. Born in 1938, as a young man he entered the Kaunas seminary, but this training was interrupted by three years of obligatory service in the Soviet army, during which his vocation was confirmed. On his return to the seminary he became involved in a Eucharistic movement run by a Jesuit that attempted to build community between priests and laity as a way of resisting Communist pressure. In 1968 Tamkevičius secretly became a Jesuit; during a long spiritual retreat that year he heard Soviet planes overhead as they flew to crush the Dubček regime in Czechoslovakia.

Because he had a youth following, the Ministry for Religion transferred him from one remote country parish to another. Then, because his name headed the signatories of a protest to Moscow against restrictions on the Kaunas seminary, for almost two years he was prohibited, as mentioned, from functioning as a priest.

In 1972 the self-immolation of a nineteen-year-old Kaunas student, Romas Kalanta, who invoked freedom for Lithuania as he burned, made a strong impact, as did the brutal repression of the demonstrations which followed. This, and the earlier imprisonment of a Jesuit for teaching the catechism, were the context for the establishment of *The Chronicle of the Catholic Church in Lithuania,* for which Tamkevičius organized a nationwide network to gather information.

In 1978, with Alfonsas Svarinskas and some other priests, Tamkevičius also founded the unofficial but public Committee for the Defense of Believers' Rights, which issued documents on religious persecution and criticized the restrictive Regulation on Religious Associations. Lithuanian Catholics were insistently demanding that the state honor its constitution.

Svarinskas was arrested and tried for, among other things, the founding of the committee. As Svarinskas was being sentenced on May 6, 1983, Tamkevičius, who had spoken in his defense, was arrested in court and, after a four day trial, was condemned to six years in a labor camp and four years of exile. He spent most of his sentence in the Urals but was transferred seven times. His legs were damaged by the cold and damp in a camp in Siberia even though he worked mainly in its kitchen and infirmary. In the labor camps he continued to hear confessions and, with the fermented juice of raisins and portions of buns, celebrated Mass.

As he feared he would never be released, Tamkevičius did not give an immediate answer when authorities offered to free him if only he would sign a confession. Some prisoners had agreed, confessing even before television cameras. After thought and prayer Tamkevičius refused just as he refused a later offer of release, without confession, provided he would leave for Western Europe.

In prison in Tomsk in 1988, he was given the choice of a common room or a solitary cell and chose the latter. "I've spent enough time looking at criminals' faces and hearing their talk," he explained in a letter to a friend; "My cell is smaller than a monk's. There's a draft of air, but no voracious fleas: not bad at all, one could make a retreat here."

Next, he was sent to a prison farm, where he had to share a hut with two nonhostile drunkards. "The table and floor were covered with potato peelings, rubbish, and cigarette butts."

In that same year, 1988, he was released after serving five and a half years of his ten-year sentence. He said that he did not bear any hate against those who had imprisoned him. On returning home he found that his parishioners had kept fresh flowers in his confessional throughout his absence.

Kazimierz Swiatek's nose, red and thickened, suggests he may be too fond of vodka. But the burst veins are due, instead, to the agonizing cold of an Arctic circle forced-labor camp where he was an inmate. His legs were frozen too, but they recovered. Swiatek spent a total of ten years in Soviet prisons and work camps.

The elder of two sons, Swiatek was born of Polish parents in Estonia on October 21, 1914. Shortly after his birth, the family moved to Pinsk, which at that time was in Poland. Young Kazimierz wanted to be a soldier but, on a visit to the Pinsk cathedral, put his hand on the tomb of Bishop Zygmunt Lozinski asking for the grace of constancy. "I received so much grace," he says wryly, "that I decided to become a priest."

In 1939 he graduated from the local seminary and was working in a parish about 100 miles distant when Russian forces reached Pinsk, where they immediately fired at the largest church's bell tower. As Ryszard Kapuściński recounted in *Imperium,* a drunken gunner shouted, "Look! We're firing at your God! And what does he do? Nothing! Not a peep out of him! Is he afraid, or what?"

Arrested by the K.G.B., Swiatek was imprisoned in death row in a jail in Brest, but when German forces invaded the Soviet Union he took advantage of the confusion to escape. The guards did not have time to kill the prisoners as they did, for instance, in Lviv by throwing grenades into their cells.

He set out for his parish, but German troops captured him. Marched with Russian prisoners-of-war towards a concentration camp, Swiatek escaped and reached his parish to find that the Gestapo occupied his presbytery. The only priest in an extensive area, Swiatek was able to resume pastoral work; for the Germans, the fact that he had been a prisoner of the Russians was in his favor. But Swiatek's odyssey was not over.

When the Red Army returned in 1944, he was arrested once more and imprisoned in Minsk beneath the K.G.B. building, then sentenced to ten years' forced labor. He spent two years in Marwinsk, Siberia, and eight in a camp in Vorkuta, close to the Arctic Circle. For some time he worked as a coal-miner (the mines had ice-covered walls, ice-covered machinery, scanty lighting and, underfoot, black mud oozed) but mostly as a timber-cutter in the woods, where it was so cold that, if one spat, the spittle froze before it reached the ground. Sometimes his legs were so swollen with cold that he could not remove his trousers.

Kapuściński has written that the cold, which reached minus forty degrees fahrenheit, was not a penetrating chill but a sharp pain that made legs and arms hurt so much they could not be touched and that the gulag inmates were "tormented, defenseless, half-naked, chronically-hungry people, exhausted to the limits and prey to the most sophisticated torture."

Hunger tortured prisoners as much as did the cold: the authorities did not want to waste food or bullets on the inmates but to kill them by degrees. Swiatek, who loves dogs, cared for a puppy which had wandered into the camp, until one day, on return from work, another prisoner asked if he would like some meat: his dog had been killed and cooked. To prevent scurvy, prisoners ate even the grass that grew around the camp. Each morning they were given ten ounces of bread before walking four and a half miles to their work site: those who did not meet the set work quotas received an ounce and a half less the next day. Swiatek dreamed of being able to eat as much bread as he wanted. Not only were the prison guards harsh, but common criminals were allowed to bully political prisoners like Swiatek. Nevertheless, he heard confessions and celebrated Mass for other prisoners, using a small ceramic chalice.

Even though any initiative was dangerous, Swiatek and other Poles in his barracks, which held over a hundred prisoners, decided to celebrate Christmas in the Polish fashion: Gospel readings, carols, a meatless meal, and the blessing of unconsecrated bread which is exchanged with best wishes. Swiatek fasted for three days to have enough bread for this *Wigilia.*

At about eleven that night the barracks doors burst open and the chief guard entered with two armed men, who drew guns on Swiatek. As they had the power to shoot the participants for far less than this initiative, it was a tense moment. Swiatek offered the blessed bread to the chief guard. Further seconds passed, then the guard turned on his heel and left. The next day, Swiatek was transferred to another gulag. The system, designed to dehumanize, degrade, and exploit inmates, could not tolerate the emergence of leaders. "I never doubted I'd leave the gulags alive," said Swiatek, who saw many inmates die, "because of my faith, which was essential for survival."

After completing his ten-year sentence, in 1954 Swiatek returned to Pinsk, which at that time had about 50,000 inhabitants. As he approached the cathedral, which he expected to be deserted if not destroyed, he saw a gleam of light from within. He found about twenty aged people listening to a layman reading the Gospel. A stole lay on the altar. For Swiatek, who had survived the hell of the gulags, it was close to heaven. He was so affected that he cried.

Swiatek, again the only priest in the zone, cautiously resumed pastoral work and prayed constantly to Bishop Zygmunt Lozinski (1870–1932), the first bishop of Pinsk, who is now being considered for beatification, to inspire vocations.

One Sunday a local tourist guide, who had never been in a church, entered the cathedral with a Russian group. After listening to Swiatek's homily the young guide decided to become a priest.

"I've been praying for you for years," Swiatek said when the youth approached him. The guide began to study Latin, the Bible, and theology secretly with Swiatek, while waiting ten years until permission was granted to enter the seminary in

Riga, Latvia. The Catholic Church in the borderlands between Poland and the Soviet Union was putting forth new shoots.

———

For twenty-six years up to 1990, Volodymyr Sterniuk lived in one room at 30 Shadlova Street in the West Ukraine capital Lviv. It was his study, bedroom, reception room, and chapel. There also he looked after a neighbor's mentally-retarded son: Sterniuk had medical training and had worked as a nurse. Tubby, short, with pince-nez glasses, white beard, and goatee like a stereotype "Mittel European" professor, Sterniuk was the highest-ranking resident prelate of a Church which had led a clandestine existence for over forty years—the Ukrainian Catholic Church, 4 to 5 million strong, which had been absorbed by the Russian Orthodox in 1946.

To avoid arrest at that time Sterniuk, a Redemptorist priest who had studied at Louvain University in Belgium in the 1930s, obtained employment as a librarian at the University of Lviv. But the following year, K.G.B. agents knocked on his door in the middle of the night: he was condemned to five years in a labor camp near Archangel in the Arctic Circle. There he worked as a lumberman but, with prudence, continued his priestly ministry; most Sunday evenings he managed to celebrate Mass in his hut with a few drops of wine and bread crusts.

At the end of the five years he was allowed to return to Pustomyty, his native village, but not to Lviv (his father had been the parish priest of Pustomyty—in the Ukrainian Catholic Church married men can be ordained priests, although priests cannot marry after ordination). By day Volodymyr worked as a forestry guard but at night was a clandestine pastor. His lodgings were searched five times. Police took a Chinese liquor glass he used as a chalice, telling him this was necessary precisely because he did not use it to get drunk.

He became a clerk in the forestry guards' office and then an assistant bookkeeper in a sawmill, where he found he had also to do a lot of sawing. The workload brought him near to a nervous breakdown. On a friend's advice, he found employment as a hospital orderly. After a correspondence course, he qualified as a medical assistant and helped at many births, each time baptizing the infant. In his spare time he taught catechism, said Mass, and heard confessions, either in his room, in friends' houses, or in the woods.

One day in July 1964, Bishop Wasyl Welychkowskyj arrived from Siberia to consecrate the fifty-seven-year-old Redemptorist as a bishop, who continued to live in his cramped second-floor apartment above a paint shop. As all his books and even his rosary had been sequestered in police raids, he wrote liturgical, moral, and dogmatic theology texts for aspirant priests, who copied them. From 1965, he ordained five or six priests annually; in 1986 police broke into a house where Sterniuk was ordaining four priests, but no action was taken, perhaps because it would have shown that the supposedly nonexistent Church was still active.

At sixty, the medical assistant Sterniuk was pensioned off with the equivalent of $7 a month. Without employment he felt more vulnerable as a clandestine bishop. He heard a little about the Vatican Council from Vatican Radio broadcasts, but they were often jammed. Initially the Vatican knew little more about Sterniuk than his name, but more must have been learned, for in 1983 he became archbishop and the representative in Lviv for Cardinal Myroslav Lubachivsky, the head of the Ukrainian Catholic Church, who resided in Rome. He made his first public appearance as a bishop only in January 1990. Although his spectacles gave him a shrewd professional air, he liked to joke. Sometimes the jokes had a sting in the tail: asked in 1990 if he would host John Paul II, he said there was not space in his room but that Gorbachev could provide it. Like many Ukrainian Catholics, he considered the Vatican far too accommodating with the Soviet authorities and the Russian Orthodox.

———

Has there ever been a cardinal before Alexandru Todea who escaped twice from prison and the second time hid from police for two years? In March 1945, he was imprisoned after commemorating the anniversary of Pius XII's election, but he escaped. He was arrested again on October 14, 1948, when he refused a police order that, like other Eastern-rite Catholic priests, he sign a declaration of adherence to the Romanian Orthodox Church and abjuration of the pope. When he was brought to the police station, the door was left open. One policeman went to inform his superiors of Todea's arrival while the other, who was to guard him, answered the telephone. On their return they found Todea had taken advantage of the open door.

For two years, in Reghin, where he was born in 1912, he lived with a family of three (a widow, her sister, and the sister's husband) in a one-room apartment. Todea slept in the kitchen, where he kept his typewriter and letters. He rarely left the apartment, as monthly an arrest warrant for him was issued. But on November 19, 1950, after receipt of a message, he went to Bucharest, where, in the cathedral sacristy, he was secretly consecrated archbishop of Blaj.

With the help of other clandestine priests, Todea reorganized the Blaj archdiocese. In his friends' apartment, he had a hole cut in the floor near the front door and constructed a hideout, not so much to avoid arrest as to have somewhere to retire if visitors came. There was barely room for him to stand in the cone-shaped cubby hole. After two years, at about midday on January 30, 1951, the Securitate (internal security) police caught up with him. Todea dived for his cubby hole in such haste that he went in head first and stuck there. "It was as if I were in a womb," he recalled. Todea, a silver-haired, rosy-complexioned man with a ready, dimpled smile, laughed when recounting certain prison episodes, a walk of a hundred miles to escape deportation, or his spell in the cubby hole.

The Securitate agents could not find the well-disguised hideout. They settled down to play cards: Todea could hear them stop whenever there was a noise. After midnight, an officer from Bucharest joined them, and at 2:30 A.M. they found the cubby hole. With guns at the ready, the Securitate police arrested the upside-down bishop as "an enemy of the people." "If the people were here," Todea responded, "they'd have no doubt who are their enemies."

"My mouth was dry," Todea recalled, "but circulation returned to my feet within three minutes."

Taken to Bucharest after his arrest on January 31, 1951, he was the object of a thirteen-month-long inquiry. Once he was summoned for interrogation by the notorious Securitate General Alexandru Nicolski, who as head of Pitesti prison had pioneered brainwashing techniques. "In the twentieth century nobody dies for their faith," said Nicolski, "you priests must be here to spy for the Anglo-Americans, so that when they invade Romania you can supervise the killing of Communists."

"Could I call a psychiatrist," replied Todea, "to check whether I'm mad or you are?"

Marched to another room and ordered to stand on one foot with both hands raised until he signed an abjuration of his Catholicism, he prayed, "Madonna, help my foot." The guard told Todea he could stand on both feet except when he, the guard, gave a warning cough. After five hours and no signature, Todea was allowed to return to his cell.

Todea was the thirteenth of a farmer's sixteen children. After studying with French Assumptionist fathers in Blaj, in 1933 he was sent to Rome's Propaganda Fide College. On graduating in theology he returned to Romania but only after doing a deal with Jesus. "Don't let me return home," Todea prayed, "unless I will remain true to all my promises." (This was to be his consolation in prison.) Shortly after his return home in 1940, Todea became secretary to the head of the Eastern-rite Catholic Church, which has the same liturgy as the Orthodox Church but recognizes the pope's authority.

On Stalin's orders, in 1946 the Eastern-rite Catholic Church in Ukraine was absorbed by the Orthodox Church; the same occurred to its counterpart in Romania in 1948 and to that in Czechoslovakia the following year. The 1,800 priests of the Eastern-rite Catholic Church in Romania were given three days to accept the new arrangement or be arrested. Of the 651 priests in Todea's diocese, 250 became Orthodox and 401 refused. Of these, 300 were arrested and 101 went underground. The proportions were roughly the same in other dioceses.

At the conclusion of the thirteen-month-long inquiry Todea was given a life sentence "for constituting a threat to the new style of life which brings happiness to the people." He became prisoner number fifty-one in the jail in Sighut near the Soviet border. In his cell, which measured about six yards by six, were five other bishops and eight priests. Todea was immediately made head of the prison cleaners. With broom in hand he was to hear many confessions. On religious feast days, the bishops and priests had to work from 4 A.M. to prevent any clandestine ceremonies. Later he was transferred to other prisons. Among the punishments he underwent for taking care of prisoners' spiritual needs was standing in the summer sun for days on end without a drink.

When the 1956 Hungarian Revolution took place, he was in Rîmnicu-Sărat prison, where he spent a total of three years in solitary confinement. "I was hosed down as were other priests," said Todea, "as if we were responsible for the uprising."

As punishment was being meted out, guards sometimes jeered, "Why doesn't your pope come to Romania to help you?"

"He will," Todea would promise, "you can be sure, he will."

In 1964 Bishop Todea was told he would be released after fourteen years in prison provided he gave a talk to the other prisoners in which he admitted his mistakes and also promised to leave the country for good. "I refused," said Todea; "I knew that Romania had to release political prisoners and prisoners of conscience to gain international recognition."

In fact, despite his refusal, in midyear he was released with a warning that he must not resume work as a priest. He did so, however, on his return to Reghin. Civil authorities offered him a job as an accountant, but he declined, suspecting that they wanted to denounce him for misappropriation of funds. He offered to teach Latin but was not accepted. Mentioning that he had been a cleaner, he requested employment as a street sweeper but was told that he was not the type for this work. He protested that in a Communist society all should be ready to do all jobs.

He was left, instead, to his own devices. Among other priestly tasks, he responded to requests from far and wide to conduct funeral services. After a funeral in 1989 for a well-known philosopher, Ioan Nicles, attended by people from all over Romania, he was arrested for the eighth and last time. Reminded that he was not allowed to act as a priest, he replied: "If families have the courage to ask me to do so, I'm not frightened enough to refuse. If you want to stop me, put me back in prison."

He was held for only six hours. A government official later told Todea there had been reluctance to arrest him for fear of adverse reaction from the West. At long last the end of both the Ceauşescu regime and of the suppression of the Eastern-rite Catholic Church were at hand.

———

When the charge of corrupting students was brought against Doina Cornea it was probably little consolation that a similar charge had been made against Socrates. It caused the expulsion of the petite lecturer in French culture from the University of Cluj in 1983, when she was in her mid fifties. Was she advocating the behavior described in libertine French novels, or the ideas of the Marquis De Sade? No, she was forced out because she urged students and staff to seek the truth and to study non-Marxist philosophers.

Doina Cornea retired to her apartment in a tree-lined street of Cluj (300,000 inhabitants), the capital of that part of Transylvania which before World War I had been a Hungarian province. But she did not retire to private life, even though her husband was not in good health. She began a letter campaign against Nicolae Ceauşescu's plan to destroy 7,000 of Romania's 13,000 villages by the end of the century and to shift millions of peasants into tower blocks in agricultural and industrial complexes.

In her letters, sometimes signed together with others, Cornea emphasized the moral and spiritual values of Romanian village life and history. She argued that the peasants' communities, churches, cemeteries, and soil were a unity signifying a "stable existence and an instinctive relationship between man and God." As they had withstood Tartar and Turkish invasions, she wrote, they should not be destroyed at the whim of a dictator. In letters to Ceauşescu she told him he was inflicting hunger, disease, and cold. In letters which could not be published in Romania but were broadcast from Munich by Radio Free Europe, she challenged Romanians, particularly intellectuals, to abandon compromise, opportunism, and hypocrisy and to live instead by Christian values.

Doina is an Eastern-rite Catholic; one of her teachers was Alexandru Todea. When the Church continued to exist clandestinely after the governmental ban, the government changed tactics and encouraged Eastern-rite Catholics to attend Latin-rite Catholic churches. Doina Cornea wrote to John Paul II arguing that the government wanted to see the Eastern-rite

Church absorbed precisely because it had courageously sustained a cultural tradition incompatible with state control.

In 1987, she and her son, Leontin Juhas, were imprisoned for handing out leaflets in support of striking workers in Brasov, many of whom had been killed by police. On release, she was held virtually incommunicado: a Securitate police van was parked permanently at the end of her street; she received death threats by phone; and police intimidated friends who tried to contact her. She was allowed out only under the escort of guards, who twice beat her up.

In protest, she went on a hunger strike in autumn 1989. When Ceauşescu was overthrown in December that year, there was one woman among the members of the National Salvation Front who appeared on television screens worldwide. She had a woolen beanie over her dark hair: it was Doina. At that moment it seemed that the causes for which she had fought had triumphed.

————

Two of the Albanians who fled across the Adriatic to Italy in 1990 spoke of Simon Jubani. In a refugee camp near Brindisi, in time off from watching television while awaiting work opportunities, they told of a priest who had stood up unflinchingly to repeated torture in a prison they shared.

Simon had been a twenty-year-old seminarian when the Communists came to power in 1946 and closed the seminary. After studying medicine for a year, Simon completed twenty-seven months of obligatory military service, during which he participated in an attempt to overthrow the Greek regime. He then worked as a nurse. He had a strong constitution and kept fit as a soccer player and athlete, which probably helped him later to resist prison torture.

Still feeling called to the priesthood, Simon consulted a bishop. He followed the bishop's advice to keep working but to study theology at night with others who were preparing themselves secretly for ordination. After ordination, he worked for six years as a clandestine priest but eventually was discovered and thrown into a small, lightless cell.

Albanian Communists had been hostile to religion from the time they gained power at the end of World War II; but, after declaring Albania officially atheist in 1967, they stepped up attempts to eliminate God from the life of the Muslim majority, the Orthodox (17 percent), and the Catholics (10 percent). Indeed, it was feared that all the Catholic hierarchy and clergy would be killed. (The last known killing of a priest was in 1988—he was guilty of baptizing a baby.)

Common criminals were put in Simon's cell to rough him up, but he won them over. He wrote frequently to Enver Hoxha, the dictator who ruled this last Stalinist stronghold, to denounce the damage he was doing, even though the letters brought further punishment.

Following Hoxha's death in 1987, international pressure won Simon's release, after twenty-five years in prison, along with that of other priests; but he was warned not to carry out priestly functions. He lived with his brother-in-law in Shkodër, a northern city of 300,000 which is the capital of Albanian Catholicism. Despite the warning, he administered the sacraments in the homes of the faithful, usually at night.

He was baptizing a baby in his brother-in-law's house in November 1990 when a friend arrived to say that the thousands of Catholics gathered at the nearby cemetery for All Souls Day wanted a Mass. Throughout Communist Europe, Catholics fell back on their cemeteries when it was impossible to attend their churches; for instance in Kishinev, the capital of Moldova, beneath the cemetery chapel Catholics secretly dug catacombs where they celebrated Mass.

In Shkodër, the neoclassical cemetery chapel was locked but intact, whereas all the city's churches had been adapted for purposes such as sport or storage. The crosses and sculpted angels on tombs had been smashed by troops or hooligans. The cemetery inspired somber memories: just beyond its walls, in sight of mountains, many had been shot by Communist execution squads. The shots, a volley, and then a single coup de grace could be heard in the city. On March 4, 1946, two Jesuit priests had been killed there. One was an Albanian, Daniel Dajani, forty, rector of the Shkodër seminary, and the other an Italian, Giovanni Fausto, forty-six, deputy provincial of the Jesuits in Albania.

Catholics continued to go to the cemetery to be near those sleeping in the Lord; despite the memories it inspired and the dilapidated tombs, the space and the trees gave a sense of peace. On All Souls Day 1990, there was also a sense of excitement and challenge: with the regime showing signs of uncertainty, Catholics were willing to risk celebration of a public Mass for the first time in decades.

White-haired Simon, who despite his years in prison still looked athletic, hurried to the cemetery and with a table brought to the chapel porch to serve as an altar, he celebrated Mass. Afterwards, youths formed a bodyguard to protect him from possible arrest. As a further precaution, he slept in a different house each night for the next week. But the feared reprisal did not come. The next Sunday, before another huge congregation, he again said Mass in the cemetery. Police watched but did not intervene. It was tacit permission for the Church to operate once again in public and proof that, although only about thirty aged priests and one sick bishop survived, the faith had lived on in many families more than two decades after Hoxha had declared Albania godless.

———

Miloslav Vlk was born to an unmarried mother in a Bohemian village in 1932; he was six when his mother married his father, a farmer. While attending school, Miloslav—or Mila, as he is still called—was also a cowherd on the family's seven and a half acres and at the age of twelve plowed all the land while his father was ill. Once, while herding cows, he spotted an airplane; this lifted his heart, and he decided to become a pilot. To acquire the necessary education he entered a seminary but then chose, instead, to be a "sky pilot." He was to be a wolf—this is the meaning of Vlk—in pastor's clothing. While at the seminary, he dared to write a rebuttal of Stalin's claim that the invented language Esperanto alienates people from their homelands.

When the Communist government closed the seminary, Vlk was excluded from university studies because he was not a member of the Communist Youth League. For some months he worked in a factory before completing two years of obligatory military service. Corporal Vlk had such a good record that, with a subterfuge, he managed to enroll in an archivist's course in the philosophy faculty of Prague University. He participated in prayer and study meetings with other Catholics.

"Ours seemed meetings of partisans or conspirators behind enemy lines," Vlk has recalled. "During them someone always kept a lookout. It was a period of extraordinary grace: despite the hostile atmosphere, God's closeness filled us with joy."

Mila had a girlfriend and wondered if, because it seemed impossible to complete his seminary studies, he should marry; but eventually he told her he had to become a priest. As he was not allowed to reenter a seminary, he worked as an archivist and also published scholarly articles on medieval history. In the slightly more tolerant atmosphere of 1963, he entered Litoměřice Seminary but found it full of Communist informers, including the rector. Lack of trust within the seminary was a factor that persuaded Mila to put all his trust in Christ.

He was tempted to leave for the West but found that some medical doctors of the Italian-founded lay movement, the Focolare, were devoting their lives to Central and Eastern Europe. Attending Focolare meetings in East Germany, he was impressed by their emphasis on the importance of community and acceptance of all setbacks and suffering as proof of God's love. The movement shaped him more than the seminary.

In 1968 he was ordained, became a bishop's secretary, and established many small ecclesial communities. But when the brief Prague spring was nipped in the bud, Vlk, who was attracting young people through initiatives such as guitar Masses, was transferred to a mountain village where state surveillance was maintained. After sixteen months, the Communist authorities ordered his transfer to another village, where he introduced himself as a Vlk/Wolf from the Bohemian forest, adding however that he did not bite.

In September 1978, his state license was withdrawn for the crime of teaching children catechism. After working for some months in a nail-and-screw factory, he left for Prague, where he found work as a window cleaner and, together with three young Slovak men, established a Focolare community in an apartment. Every now and again his window cleaning was interrupted by security police interrogations, which, with his archivist training, he carefully recorded in full detail. The interrogations did not stop him from doing pastoral work clandestinely. After a heart attack in 1987, he had to reduce his activities; he obtained work as a bank archivist.

At the beginning of 1989 he was allowed to resume his priestly ministry in a remote village where there was not even a telephone. It seemed that he had been becalmed for almost a decade, but as Communism crumbled his life was about to accelerate.

———

The Slovak pronunciation of his name is close to "courage." This is appropriate, as Ján Chryzostom Korec proved courageous in and out of prison. In 1991 he became Cardinal

Korec, an extraordinarily swift ascent for a man who had been an elevator repairman only two years earlier.

"My life is like a novel," said "Cardinal Courage" when interviewed in Nitra in February 1990; "I'm not used to all this." He gestured towards the paintings in their gilt frames, the wood sculptures, and the fine wallpaper of his spacious study. He had not had time to become used to the episcopal residence as he had arrived only the previous night. The study was well appointed largely because the previous resident, a vicar-general, had been head of the diocesan branch of Pacem in Terris, the government-sponsored priests' peace organization. This had ensured him certain privileges, but he had now been assigned to a parish near the Polish border.

Ján Korec was dapper, wearing a light grey suit and red-framed spectacles. Although grey-haired, he looked younger than sixty-five, yet he had suffered tuberculosis and spent eight years in prison.

He was born in January 1924 in Bosany, Slovakia, one of three children whose parents both worked in a tannery. In 1939 he was about to begin an apprenticeship in the Bata shoe firm but instead accepted an opportunity to become a Jesuit novice. Korec was a student of theology in 1950 when the government suppressed all religious orders, and like thousands of others was transferred from one monastery-jail to another. Released for health reasons, he became an assistant to the accountant of a machine tool firm, the first of a number of occupations.

That same year he was ordained secretly in a hospital by an arrested bishop who pretended to be sick so that he could perform the ceremony. Ten months later, the government had all bishops arrested; and even though he had studied theology for only one year, Ján Korec was one of those secretly ordained as a replacement bishop. He was twenty-seven, the world's youngest Catholic bishop. He had misgivings: he felt not only that he was too young but also that he was timid and scholarly rather than a leader. Moreover, he considered the substitute head of his Jesuit province too precipitate in ordaining Jesuits who had not completed their training.

While secretly preparing and ordaining priests, Korec worked in the Tatrachema factory of Bratislava, which made products such as floor and shoe polish. His health had always been delicate; breathing chemical fumes and lugging heavy drums from a heated interior to a freezing yard damaged his lungs. After three years he obtained a job in the Institute for Work Hygiene, first as a clerk, then archivist. He had never hidden that he was a Christian but had not disclosed that he was a Jesuit and a bishop. He was constantly tailed and spied upon. A Communist colleague, who did not know Korec was a priest, suggested that he marry to allay suspicions. Police broke into Korec's tiny room in an apartment where he lodged with a family, to confiscate his books and notes.

In 1960, with other Jesuits, he was arrested and accused of aiding religious activities, maintaining contact with enemy powers (the Vatican), and being a lackey of imperialism. At the memory of it he laughed: "Imagine what a capitalist I was when I worked in a chemical factory hauling heavy drums out into the cold. All day long I was coughing from tuberculosis. The son of parents who had always worked in a tannery, I was sentenced by a judge who, I'm sure, knew the working class only from books."

The sentence was twelve years at Valdice, northern Bohemia, where 200 priests and 6 bishops were imprisoned. One who particularly impressed Korec was Bishop Ján Vojtaššák: at the age of eighty-two, he was serving a twenty-four-year sentence in Czechoslovakia's harshest prison. There he received his invitation to the Vatican Council but was not allowed to go. With other priests, Korec was assigned to the section for hardened criminals. At one time there were only four lavatories for 180 prisoners, at another only one shower for 1,500: the prisoners were allowed only one brief shower each week. Korec counseled some fellow prisoners and, after his release, helped a few obtain revision of their trials. On request, he gave religious instruction while, for instance, washing the stairs or wrote it on cigarette paper for delivery in a matchbox. One of his prison tasks was to produce frosted glass in unhygienic conditions; those who did not meet constantly rising quotas were punished.

Korec discovered that the substitute Jesuit head of his province, who had been too hasty about having priests ordained, had disclosed that he (Korec) had ordained some. Under interrogation in prison, Korec admitted what the interrogators already knew and willingly engaged in discussing religion but refused to give any further information. On one occasion, after three weeks without having had anything to report, the interrogator used the "put yourself in my shoes, I'm only doing my job, so collaborate" argument.

"You want me to tell you the truth?" asked the prisoner.

"Yes. Do."

"But don't get angry."

"No, go ahead."

"I wouldn't do your job for all the money in the world." The interrogator rose and, with his back to Korec, his hands in his pockets, stared out of the window. That was the end of the interrogation.

While in solitary confinement, Korec developed a survival routine based on the Jesuit Spiritual Exercises. Each morning he spent an hour in meditation, then said Mass. After Mass he recalled texts in theology and philosophy, discussing them aloud as if undergoing an examination. If he tired he sang hymns and folk songs before resuming study and prayer. On return to a common cell he felt he had benefited from a spiritual renewal course. In prison, seminarians were given theology lessons in the exercise yard, were examined there, and were eventually ordained.

Imagination was a great resource for Korec: as he had cycled across the bridge over the Danube for the 6 A.M. shift at the Tatrachema factory in Bratislava, he had thought of his spiritual union with a Jesuit friend who was a missionary in Rhodesia and with other Jesuits working in the Andes or teaching in universities. In prison, a present of a packet of figs from Smyrna transported him in imagination to that city of St. Paul and St. Polycarp.

With the advent of Alexander Dubček's government in 1968 Korec was released, rehabilitated, and treated in a tuberculosis clinic. Allowed to visit Rome, he was granted a papal audience; he asked if he should dress as a street cleaner, as he had no episcopal robes. Paul VI gave him his regalia from his time as archbishop of Milan. On Korec's return home, customs officials wanted to impound the regalia but desisted when Korec told them it would make them a laughing stock worldwide.

Hostilities against religion resumed after the Warsaw Pact armies' invasion of Czechoslovakia. Korec worked as a municipal garbage man, then as a maintenance mechanic, storekeeper, and railway porter. In 1974 his rehabilitation was canceled, and he was imprisoned again to serve the remaining four years of his sentence but, for health reasons, was soon released. Once more he was considered an enemy of the people and a second-class citizen. Communist authorities, who accused him of seeking martyrdom, offered him permission to work as a priest in a remote village, presumably because they wanted him as far as possible from Bratislava, the capital. He declined, saying he would accept only if other priests under constraint were allowed to minister without state controls.

Employed or unemployed, he was organizing the semiclandestine Church throughout Slovakia. One layman said that, as an underground bishop, Korec was the "leading moral authority in Slovakia." The semiclandestine Church consisted of lay apostolic and spiritual groups, priests and sisters without government licenses, and also some licensed priests.

"We informed the official Church authorities of our activities but they didn't always want to know," Korec explained.

"Communists closed an eye to most of what we did for fear repression would drive us into political opposition. We weren't involved in politics—our aim was to deepen faith because we were convinced that the best service was to give people something substantial. We held retreats and days of contemplation, sometimes in the mountains. For forty years no religious books, apart from prayer books, were published—even books of spiritual exercises became underground publications. The reaction was a great spiritual movement—one day in 1989 about 200,000 came to a procession in Nitra: three times its total population."

To counter the dearth of religious literature, Korec wrote some sixty books, of which fifteen have been translated into other languages, ranging from biblical commentary to reflections on contemporary issues. The typescripts were sent to Canada for printing, then the volumes were smuggled back to Slovakia. On the books' covers the anonymous author was described as a "worker in overalls."

From 1976 to 1989, police interrogated the "worker in overalls" more than thirty times. He returned as a laborer to the Tatrachema factory. This made his tuberculosis flare up again, but at least he was living in slightly better circumstances in a friend's apartment; this time his room was three yards by five. To foil bugging, Korec communicated with visitors by speaking into a rubber tube which they held to their ear.

He obtained employment as an elevator repairman, which was better for his health. After the "Velvet Revolution," he was made rector of the Bratislava seminary and then, within weeks, bishop of Nitra, Central Europe's oldest diocese where the first church was established in the ninth century. He himself found his story more like fiction than fact—and that was before the epilogue of being made a cardinal.

Despite Communist hostility, Korec, like Vlk, Jubani, Cornea, Todea, Sadūnaitė, Sterniuk, Swiatek, and Tamkevičius, persisted with his apostolate. Although he considered himself timid and scholarly, like the others Korec was undaunted by imprisonment. Indeed Nijolė Sadūnaitė was reassured by imprisonment that not even the K.G.B. could destroy the best of human nature. Doina Cornea found in oppression and imprisonment the essence of liberty, even though at a terrible cost. They were reaffirming their humanity, their self-image shaped by their beliefs, by refusing to compromise. Alexandru Todea's deal with Jesus before returning home from Rome may provide a clue: he resisted because of fidelity to a commitment. For these witnesses, not only did the truth deserve to be propagated in spite of all the dangers, but some of them were able to challenge their country's leaders with it. In seemingly hopeless circumstances, their morale remained high; even in prison they held the upper ground. What was proclaimed as the march of history did not drown out the quiet voice of their consciences. All lived on into the post-Communist era, which contained bitter surprises for some and new challenges for all.

Chapter 5

Sup with a Long Spoon

When you sup with the devil, use a long spoon.
English Proverb

While Catholics suffered for their faith under European Communist regimes, the Vatican negotiated on their behalf with the governments concerned. Later, some of these Catholics were to complain that the Vatican's *Ostpolitik* (dealings with European countries under Communist regimes) did more harm than the K.G.B., because they could resist persecution but not the "Vaticanski" appointment of some pliable bishops acceptable to the regimes. They thought the Vatican should have relied on them to conserve the faith without worrying about "bringing oxygen" to the institutional Church.

An ecclesiology that took account of the experience of the Korean Church might have made this possible. Laymen brought Catholicism to Korea in the eighteenth century, and it grew initially without clergy. On the basis of that experience, the Vatican might have been less worried by the prospect of the Church in Communist Europe being deprived of clergy and being dependent on the laity living their faith in secret.

Instead, its *Ostpolitik* presumed that a hierarchy must be maintained and the Church must have a recognized public role and structure. But at the same time, by creating clandestine bishops, the Vatican prepared for the eventuality that the regimes would suppress or manipulate the official Church. The clandestine hierarchy was particularly extensive in Czechoslovakia, but this too created persistent problems: the Vatican was wary not only of the Communists playing the official Church off against the underground Church but also of the underground Church becoming a sect of zealots who felt superior to the official Church. Indeed, as Cardinal Korec's words indicate, there was an official Church, an underground Church, and a sort of semiofficial Church made up of state-licensed priests who participated in underground Church activities. The confines were hazy.

The Vatican's *Ostpolitik* had a paradoxical aspect. In the immediate postwar period, there was no Vatican desire for negotiations and little possibility of them. It was thought that European Communist regimes were not stable. Eventually negotiations began on the presumption that the regimes were stable and culminated in the John Paul II–Gorbachev meeting as Communist Europe imploded.

So strong was the bond between the czarist regime and the Russian Orthodox Church that, initially, the Vatican seems to have regarded the Bolshevik revolution with equanimity, as if convinced that conditions for Catholics could not worsen. The new government had proclaimed religious freedom, but soon alarming news of violence and antireligious measures arrived, mainly from Monsignor Achille Ratti (in 1922 he became Pius XI), who was both nuncio to Poland and apostolic visitor for Russia, although not allowed entry to that country. In May 1919 Benedict XV said that the hopes raised by the proclamation of religious liberty had been disappointed: the Vatican attempted to intercede even for Orthodox bishops but had received harsh replies from Lenin and other Soviet officials.

In response to an appeal from the Orthodox patriarch of Moscow, Tikhon, for help against famine and epidemic, in September 1922 Pius XI sent a relief mission headed by a

United States Jesuit, Father Edmund Walsh. As if to fend off criticism, Pius XI explained to the Vatican administration that this was not a recognition of the Soviet regime; he had earlier said the mission should defend the inhabitants' civil and religious rights.

In this period Soviet delegates participated for the first time at an international conference. It began in Geneva and continued in Rapallo, Italy. The Vatican tried to negotiate with them but without success; it seems the main obstacle was the Holy See's request for return of seized ecclesiastical property. Some Orthodox claim that the Vatican was trying to get Soviet agreement to Catholicism replacing Orthodoxy.

Perhaps because the attempt to negotiate broke down, the Vatican began to consecrate clandestine bishops for the Soviet Union. In Berlin in 1926 the papal nuncio, Eugenio Pacelli, secretly consecrated as bishop a French Jesuit, Michel d'Herbigny, who was head of the Pontifical Oriental Institute in Rome. D'Herbigny entered Russia and contacted a French Assumptionist priest, Pie Neveu. In 1907 Neveu had been sent to Makejevka, Ukraine, as chaplain for French and Belgian miners. As World War I was followed by revolution and then civil war, it was presumed he had perished but in 1922 his superiors heard from him again: he wrote asking for a pair of trousers and a map of the new Europe. D'Herbigny consecrated Neveu as a clandestine bishop in St. Louis Church, Moscow, within the shadow of the K.G.B. headquarters. D'Herbigny consecrated other bishops also but, for obscure reasons, fell from grace with the Vatican. He resigned as a bishop and spent his last twenty-one years confined to a Jesuit residence; he died in 1957. The clandestine bishops except Neveu were persecuted, and some were sentenced to death. For health reasons Neveu went to Paris in 1936 and was not allowed to return to the Soviet Union.

Moscow complained that the Holy See was behind "every anti-Soviet crusade" (it certainly had launched a prayer crusade for the Soviet Union). Pius XI made repeated, trenchant criticism of Communism; he said that Communists aimed to "kill faith in God so that [they] can then do whatever they want" and concluded that Communism was "intrinsically perverse."

Eugenio Pacelli, who had consecrated d'Herbigny bishop, became secretary of state to Pius XI and, as Pius XII, succeeded him in March 1939. Perhaps his attitude towards Communism was influenced by his experiences in 1919 when a Bolshevik regime was established in Munich, where he was the Vatican's representative. Militants entered the Vatican diplomatic mission and threatened Pacelli with a pistol.

"Russians headed that government," Pacelli recalled in an interview to *Le Matin* two years later. "Every idea of law, liberty, and democracy was suppressed; only the Soviet press could circulate." As pope he was as intransigent as his predecessor, although during the war he refrained from criticizing the Soviet Union. After the war, he witnessed the expansion of Soviet power and influence: Lithuania and West Ukraine, with predominantly Catholic populations, were absorbed into the Soviet Union while Communist regimes were established from East Germany to Albania, from Czechoslovakia to Bulgaria. Everywhere atheism was encouraged "to liberate people from religious prejudice," and government offices controlled even the Church's internal affairs. Within a few years, about 8,000 Catholic priests were killed, imprisoned, or deported.

Pius XII protested the trials of churchmen such as Mindszenty and Stepinac and the accompanying smear campaigns. In the early 1950s he invented the term "Church of Silence" to describe the muzzling of Christians under Communist regimes. He found peaceful coexistence an inadequate ideal, as it implied that some peoples would be segregated from the rest of the world; he was not resigned to Communist control of half Europe; and he called Yalta "the curse of our times." His aversion to any compromise with Communism induced him to keep Cardinal Stefan Wyszyński waiting days for an audience because he had reached an agreement with the Polish government. Wyszyński, who had undergone house arrest and harassment by the Communist government, was offended and humiliated.

John XXIII changed Vatican policy. His experience as the Vatican's representative in Bulgaria and his historical sense, as well as the evolution of the international situation, all played a part in this. While reaffirming the strictures against Marxism, his encyclical of May 1961, *Mater et Magistra,* noted that Catholics could collaborate with others who had a different vision "in projects which are good or could lead to good." Two years later, his last encyclical, *Pacem in terris,* distinguished between ideologies and the movements which derive from them: "Doctrines . . . do not change but the movements which act in constantly changing historical circumstances undergo their influence and cannot avoid even profound changes. Moreover who can deny that . . . there are positive elements worthy of approval in these movements? As a result it can happen that a drawing together or a meeting, which yesterday was considered not opportune or not productive, is so today or can be tomorrow."

In Italy, where there had been a Church ban on Catholic support for the Communists, the Party's vote soared in the election held a month after the encyclical appeared, and John XXIII was accused of aiding it. Similar criticism was made in other countries, including the Vatican itself: some of those who had suffered under Communist regimes had become Vatican officials, while other key curial figures still held to Pius XII's intransigence. One of the best known, Cardinal Alfredo Ottaviani, deplored those who "shook hands with persecutors." There had been no sympathy between Pius XII and Josef Stalin; but Nikita Khrushchev, energetic persecutor of Christians, liked John XXIII, who had been recommended to him by the Italian Communist leader Palmiro Togliatti. The

Ukrainian peasant appreciated the Bergamo peasant's personality and also his efforts for peace, particularly during the Cuban missile crisis. In 1961 Khrushchev sent John XXIII congratulations for his eightieth birthday and, the following year, Christmas greetings.

John XXIII wrote in his diary "Is this Krouscheff . . . or Nikita Khrushchev as he signs himself . . . preparing surprises for us? Tonight . . . I rose and knelt before my crucifix, I consecrated my life, in an extreme sacrifice of myself, for this great enterprise of the conversion of Russia to the Catholic Church."

On March 7, 1963, John XXIII received Khrushchev's daughter Rada and her husband Aleksei Adjubei, a member of the Central Committee of the Communist Party. Adjubei proposed establishment of Holy See–Soviet Union relations. John XXIII advised patience, as at that moment such a step would not be understood.

John XXIII had summoned the Vatican Council, which, he was to say, wanted to meet contemporary needs rather than "renew condemnations." Bishops from the Communist countries were invited, but would they be allowed to come? In November 1961 John XXIII had the Vatican's representative in Ankara approach the Soviet ambassador there. He, in turn, asked Khrushchev to allow Catholic bishops from the Soviet Union to attend the council. After a week, permission was granted. With that permission in hand, the nuncio in Ankara obtained from the respective embassies approval for the bishops of other European Communist countries to attend.

In September 1962 a Dutchman, Monsignor Johannes Willebrands, a key figure in the Vatican's ecumenical affairs, was sent to Moscow to explain the council's aims to Russian Orthodox authorities. It was the first official contact in Moscow in modern times between an authorized representative of the Holy See and the Russian Orthodox. The Orthodox subsequently accepted an invitation to the council.

Another who contributed to the thaw in relations between the Catholic Church and the European Communist regimes was Cardinal Franz Koenig, Archbishop of Vienna. He first entered a Communist country in 1960 when he set out for Cardinal Alojzije Stepinac's funeral in Zagreb. He did not arrive because his car slid off an ice-covered road and his jaw was broken. Rather than a few days in Yugoslavia, he spent weeks there in a hospital and concluded God was trying to tell him something; he decided to dedicate more time to Communist countries. The following year he crossed Czechoslovakia by car and, at Cieszyn, entered Poland. In Czechoslovakia, where restrictions on the Church were severe, he noted that no one dared raise a hand to wave to him, but on entering Poland a welcoming committee of hundreds greeted him with songs. A little distant stood a man in a black cassock who had accompanied the welcoming committee.

"Who's that chaplain?" Koenig asked.

"That's Karol Wojtyła," he was told, "the auxiliary bishop of Cracow."

Some Roman curialists were peeved at Koenig's autonomous initiatives, but later the Vatican assigned him unofficial missions. Its *Ostpolitik* was gathering momentum.

Its main negotiator was a short, compactly built priest, Agostino Casaroli, who had wanted to be a philosopher but became a diplomat—although for decades, because of delicate health, it seemed that he would never leave Rome on a diplomatic mission. He first worked in the Secretariat of State towards the end of Pius XI's reign. He became known as an "archive mouse" for his close study of the history of the Holy See's negotiations, and later as the "Archbishop of Lima" for his tireless polishing up of documents (a pun on the Italian word *limare,* meaning to "polish up" or "perfect"). He paid particular attention to the dealings between the Holy See and Latin American nations which had persecuted the Church but later established concordats. It stood him in good stead in prolonged negotiations leading to a concordat with the Dominican Republic. And it also made him aware that rapprochement with formerly hostile regimes tended to bring harsh criticism from those who had suffered under them.

In April 1963 Casaroli, who was number two in the Vatican Ministry of Foreign Affairs, led a Holy See delegation to Vienna for a United Nations conference on consular law. While there, he received word from John XXIII to go to Cardinal József Mindszenty in Budapest and Cardinal Josef Beran in Prague. Previously Casaroli had not had a specific interest in Central and Eastern Europe, but from now on it was to become an absorbing concern.

Seven years earlier, Mindszenty had taken refuge in the American legation in Budapest, where Cardinal Koenig had managed to see him a few weeks before Casaroli. Casaroli visited Mindszenty and also Hungarian government officials.

Next he went to Prague to meet Beran, who had been made a Hero of the Resistance after surviving the Dachau concentration camp, where he had known many Communist leaders. Despite this, he had been placed under house arrest. For fear of bugging, he communicated with Casaroli by written notes. As a result of these two trips, Beran and, somewhat later, Mindszenty reluctantly left their countries in return for permission from the authorities for the appointment of successors and for future Holy See–government negotiations.

In 1963 Paul VI (whose one diplomatic posting had been the nunciature in Warsaw in 1923, not long after the Bolshevik armies were defeated near the Vistula River) succeeded John XXIII. He developed the Holy See's *Ostpolitik,* with Casaroli as the Vatican's man in various Central and Eastern European capitals. An agreement was reached with the Hungarian government, while the Czechoslovakian regime accepted František Tomašek as apostolic administrator in Prague. A protocol of agreement was signed in Belgrade in 1966 (Yugoslavia had been the last European Communist country to break off relations with the Vatican; it did so in 1952 because Stepinac was made a cardinal).

Casaroli's visit to Poland came later amid the hierarchy's diffidence. The primate, Cardinal Wyszyński, who felt the Vatican could not really understand the situation, feared a Holy See–government agreement over the bishops' heads. Later, in a synod in Rome, he said wryly "vir casaroliensis non sum" (I'm not a Casaroli man). In Poland the Church had such authority that an agreement was not urgent.

Casaroli did not see Vatican policy merely as reaching agreements between one institution and another. He pointed out that agreements were made possible only because of the faith of Central and Eastern European Catholics and were designed to serve these communities. Casaroli, who had always devoted his spare time to disadvantaged Roman youth, was confident that the Church would appeal more than the Party to young people in Central and Eastern Europe. He admired the underground Catholics' faith but feared that, unless the Church gained recognition, they would become an elite group detached from fellow believers.

The Vatican's *Ostpolitik* has been criticized for recognition of deplorable regimes and appointment of a few stooge bishops. Certainly Cardinal László Lékai and some other Hungarian bishops were less than inspiring leaders, but Lékai was not suspect at the time of his appointment, as he had been Mindszenty's secretary. Bishop Vekoslav Grmič of Marbor, Slovenia, after having been a brilliant seminary teacher, became at least intellectually sympathetic to Communism. In 1980 the Vatican persuaded him to step down. The most notorious collaborationist-bishop was Jozef Vrana, apostolic administrator of Olomouc, Moravia, Czechoslovakia. He presided over the government-sponsored Pacem in Terris Association and managed to promote some of its members to key posts in adjoining dioceses, as they were without bishops. It is said that Vrana promised Vatican representatives that he would resign from

Pacem in Terris after his episcopal appointment but did not do so because the secret police managed to blackmail him. If so, the Vatican should have been better informed than to appoint him. He died in 1987. The fact that so many other dioceses in Czechoslovakia remained vacant because of a lack of agreement between the Vatican and the government about the proposed appointment shows that the Vatican was not prepared to accept government dupes after the experience with Vrana.

Some of the Vatican's bilateral arrangements were applied less satisfactorily than others, but they did not represent the sum total of Vatican *Ostpolitik*. The Holy See was also involved as a full member in the Helsinki Agreement on European Security and Cooperation. In 1973 Finland invited the Holy See to participate in its preparatory sessions. Some suspected the conference would merely allow the Soviet Union to obtain endorsement of the Communist Bloc frontiers, but the Holy See proposed that, to favor peace, the conference acknowledge liberty of conscience and religion as being the right of all peoples. Even the Communist Bloc countries accepted this; Cardinal Casaroli signed the agreement for the Holy See on August 1, 1975.

This proved an important factor in what has been called the "erosion of the Communist system." It was recognition of a sphere of liberty that was denied in practice. At intervals the conference reassembled in European capitals to review the situation of religion and conscience in various countries. It became an international forum in which Christians of Central and Eastern Europe could make their voice heard. And oppressed groups within these countries could always appeal to the Helsinki principles. (Albania did not sign the agreement until 1991.)

Insertion of the conscience and religion principles was a substantial success for Vatican *Ostpolitik,* which was proceeding patiently and methodically as John XXIII and Paul VI had recommended. In 1978, however, it accelerated, for in that "year of three popes" Paul VI died, John Paul I lasted only thirty-three days, and then the "chaplain" who had awaited Cardinal Koenig's arrival at the Polish border eighteen years before became John Paul II.

The news spread through Communist Europe to prisoners such as Simon Jubani in Albania and Alexandru Todea in Romania. In Prague it inspired Archbishop František Tomašek, and in Soviet Asia the news raced from one Polish community to another. In Moscow an Orthodox layman, Andrei Bessmertny, acquired a photo of the Polish pope for his apartment. At last the Church of Silence had found its voice.

Chapter 6

Karol Comes in from the Cold

In their attempt to control the Catholic Church in Central and Eastern Europe, Communists seem to have calculated everything except the possibility that a Soviet Bloc bishop become pope. Cardinal Achille Silvestrini, prefect of the Vatican Congregation for Eastern-rite Churches, has compared Communist control of the Church to that wielded by the Austro-Hungarian Empire. To reinforce their regimes, the Hapsburg emperors controlled the Church but granted it privileges. The Communists exercised control to stifle the Church. The "Catholic" emperors were shrewd enough to see the advisability of a veto over the election of any pope who could shake the empire. But the Communists had no such veto. And John Paul II was to shake the empire.

In the Vatican gardens there is now a slice of the Berlin Wall, a cement panel on which part of the facade of a grey and blue East Berlin church was painted by two artists from there shortly after their escape. Lightning streaks down the pale blue above the facade while superimposed on it are unintelligible squiggles and graffiti. The Wall fragment, about eleven by four feet and weighing two and a half tons, stands at the back of a plant nursery, opposite a food warehouse and the bastions near a museum entrance. A marble slab nearby, which records that the Wall fragment is a gift from Marco Piccinini, carries a passage from

John Paul II's inaugural homily: "Be not afraid. Open your doors to Christ, throw them wide open to his salvific dominion, open state borders and political and economic systems. Be not afraid." The cement panel in the gardens makes it seem that the hopes aroused by John Paul's words shattered the Wall.

The Wall's dismantlement could not be foreseen at the time of John Paul's election, but the election in itself indicated that something was terribly, terribly awry in the Communists' calculations. One of the breed they had boxed in with constraints had become head of a Church of over 900 million members. And not only was there to be a Polish pope in Rome but, worse still, a Roman pontiff in Poland stirring up defiance, for who could keep him out for any time? He was an icon of the Communists' failure to crush religion. Was there any way to remedy matters? The Communists must have examined Wojtyła's career for indications of his possible behavior as pope. Since being made a cardinal in 1967, he had played second fiddle to Warsaw's Cardinal Stefan Wyszyński; but this may have indicated only that he wanted to avoid any possibility of dividing the Church, rather than lack of leadership qualities. He had been an actor, wrote poetry, and taught ethics at the Catholic University of Lublin, which gave him cachet as an artist and an intellectual, two groups which rebelled against Communist authority.

Immediately after the papal election, Soviet authorities had an analyst in their Academy of Science, Oleg Bogomolov, prepare a report on John Paul II. Published for the first time in 1993, it said that John Paul was anti-Socialist (i.e., anti-Communist) but as archbishop of Cracow had used the Vatican tactic of "expansion by dialogue." As he had been a worker, Bogomolov's report continued, election of this "rightist" would be interpreted as proof of the Catholic Church's democratic tendencies. The report suggested that, as John Paul's election meant the Church could supply a moral basis for Western criticism of Communist societies over human rights, the Vatican be informed that involvement in a hostile campaign would lead to (greater) restrictions on the Church in Communist Europe. It proposed forestalling hostile pronouncements by improving relations with the Catholic clergy in Lithuania, Ukraine, and Belarus while keeping an eye on the Uniate Church in Ukraine to "block its adherence to the Catholic Church." It foresaw that John Paul would promote ecumenism and said that the Orthodox leadership should be "induced" to speak out against the Vatican's plans to reunite Christianity. Finally, it recommended that Communism emphasize its ethical-moral values because reduction of human existence to the socio-political "creates grounds for strengthening the Church's position."

Communists trying to predict John Paul's likely policy should have paid particular attention to his influence in Nowa Huta, which had been built outside Cracow as a new, godless city for the new Socialist citizen. True to their conviction that if people's material needs were met they would have no desire for religion, the Communists planned a churchless steel-producing town as a contrast to Cracow with its many churches. They built the industrial city on what had been good farming land because heavy industry was the formula for Socialist salvation. But the workers demanded churches. And their demands were backed by the archbishop of Cracow, Karol Wojtyła.

From the early 1950s, people in Nowa Huta had gathered for Mass in a house chapel. In 1957 they erected a cross near where they wanted a church. They were to wait twenty years for it, and during those years they celebrated many Masses in the open, despite icy winds that cut faces like blades. But, in the end, they obtained their church.

Police frequently harassed worshippers; in April 1960 many were injured when police attacked. Five years later, Archbishop Wojtyła obtained permission to enlarge the chapel. In

1969 he placed the church's cornerstone, a fragment from the site of St. Peter's tomb which had been sent by Paul VI. Cardinal Roger Etchegaray has described an open-air Mass on the site in midwinter that year attended by 50,000, half the town's population. Communist authorities denied that permission had been given for the church's construction, but under pressure from the workers and Wojtyła they eventually allowed it. Stones for the church were brought from all over Poland and Europe, particularly by young Germans as a sign of reconciliation. Karol Wojtyła dedicated the church to the Mother of God, Queen of Poland, in May 1977. Because of the roof's shape it is known as the ark church. Large windows ensure that it is light-filled. It has a strong, confident air, fortress as well as ark, which makes it almost possible to overlook its ugly sculptures. At the opening ceremony, Wojtyła underlined that human beings, made in God's image, cannot be manipulated as if they depended only on economic laws. He had proved that the Church was closer to the workers than was the Party which claimed to speak for them. From the Soviet viewpoint, it boded ill for his pontificate.

What boded worst of all, of course, was that, unlike his immediate predecessors, he knew life under Communism: not only the blatant persecution but what he called the "civil death" and the asphyxiating atmosphere as if a gas had penetrated all aspects of life; the enervating drabness and dullness as if stupidity reigned—Czech intellectuals were to rename Communist Czechoslovakia "Absurdistan"; the feeling that society was a facade held in place only by fear; the rhetoric about achieved social justice in contrast to the privileges of Party members; the restriction of all horizons; and the creation of a world in which the state pretended to pay, the workers pretended to work, and all were diminished.

Catholic organizations such as Aid to the Church in Need helped Central and Eastern European Christians, but it was often assumed that these aid organizations were reactionary groups supporting those who opposed progressive regimes. Some aid-organization officials averred that promoters of the Vatican *Ostpolitik* attempted to hinder such aid to Central and Eastern European Christians lest it upset negotiations with the regime.

Despite such groups and the Vatican's diplomatic efforts, many Catholics in Communist Europe said they felt they had been forgotten by their coreligionists elsewhere. It was partly a case of out of sight, out of mind: in 1975 Macmillan published Daniel Madden's *A Religious Guide to Europe.* It represented the truncated Europe which was taken for the whole in the West; only 5 of its 529 pages were devoted to Eastern Europe.

John Paul II was convinced that there was not so much a Church of Silence as a disinclination to hear its voice. He, however, would not let anyone forget it. He did not make a frontal attack on Communist regimes; instead, as in his first speech from St. Peter's, he appealed for individuals to be fearless and insisted on the right to religious liberty and on peoples' sovereign rights. This carried a particular weight because he was Polish. The Italian popes who had preceded him did not have such a strong national coloring. When John Paul II spoke of a people's right to respect for their national, cultural, and religious traditions, it was a Pole as well as a pope speaking. His words applied universally, but they were also a challenge to the status quo in Poland.

His words were also heard elsewhere in Communist Europe. The Hungarian primate Cardinal László Lékai aimed at reaching partial agreements with the government and refrained from criticizing it. He maintained that his cautious step-by-step approach was in line with Paul VI's *Ostpolitik* but Cardinal Wyszyński had been critical of him, and John Paul II favored more vigorous advocacy of religious and human rights. Admittedly, Hungarian Catholicism was weaker than Polish and not only because Catholics there were only 60 percent of the population as against 90 percent in Poland. But Lékai seemed too complacent about the status quo: indeed, he rashly said that the Communists had realized the Church's social teaching. He detached the Church from whatever ferment there was in society. John Paul II's election meant that Hungarian Catholics critical of their primate were reassured there would be life after Lékai; moreover, Hungary, where the first successes of Vatican *Ostpolitik* were registered, came to be regarded as an example of its pitfalls.

John Paul strengthened the Church's resistance to the particularly harsh regime in Czechoslovakia, which had outlawed 10,000 religious, imprisoned bishops, and denied licenses to minister for many priests. Once the license was withdrawn, priests had to find work or be arrested for "parasitism." Catholic schools were closed, Church landholdings and property were confiscated, and Church publications were suppressed. The Czechoslovakian government also had more success than others in establishing a stooge Priests for Peace movement, later called Pacem in Terris, which was a mouthpiece for the government on both internal and international affairs. Some probably joined out of a belief that the Church could survive only by cooperating with the state, others because membership ensured privileges. Another factor was that ethnic Hungarians in Slovakia believed Pacem in Terris could repair what they felt was discrimination against them.

In 1967 in the spa town of Karlovy Vary, the founder of the Priests for Peace movement, tall, heavily-built Monsignor Jozef Plojhár, attended the first Christian-Marxist dialogue held in a Communist country. Although as Minister for Health he had legalized abortion, he had an honorary degree from the Litoměřice Faculty of Theology, which showed how far the rot had spread. At Karlovy Vary, Plojhár wore a clergyman's grey suit with a cerise shirt taut over a paunch, which suggested that he had always eaten only too well. Cardinal Casaroli made a similar notation on meeting the government-appointed vicar-capitular of Prague in 1963: "he made a painful impression, well-built and well-nourished, he seemed unconcerned about the situation and the government of the diocese."

In 1971, under Gustáv Husák's government, Plojhár revived his stooge organization but this time called it the Pacem in Terris Association instead of Priests for Peace. Archbishop František Tomašek attended its first meetings but subsequently advised his priests against joining.

The son of a teacher, Tomašek was born in Moravia in 1899, when it was a province of the Austro-Hungarian Empire, and entered a seminary in 1918, the year in which Czechoslovakia gained independence to the cry of "Away from Vienna, Away from Rome." In 1934 he became an assistant professor of pedagogy and catechetics; after the war, he resumed teaching these subjects. In 1949 he was made a bishop in secret and did parish work; the following year he was arrested along with other bishops and was condemned to three years in a labor camp. He was allowed to do parish work again for a decade until 1963, when the Communists approved his appointment as apostolic administrator of Prague to replace Jozef Beran.

It must have seemed to them they had benefited by the change. Beran was uncompromising, but nothing in the past of pious, tranquil Tomašek suggested he would give them trouble: he seemed the ideal choice to preside over the euthanasia of the Czechoslovak Church. So this blue-eyed Monsignor Five-by-Five, with an aureole of curly hair, short but sturdy as an oak, was installed in the archbishop's palace (later used for Milos Forman's film *Amadeus*). The palace stands just outside the gates of Hradčany Castle, which dominates Prague and is the seat of civil government. Significantly, the cathedral of St. Vitus is within the castle complex, a pointer to a Church-state embrace which long preceded Communism. Sometimes Tomašek found the Communists had shut him out of the cathedral. Moreover they were present in the episcopal palace even when not visible; it was staffed mainly by internal security agents, and Tomašek found his study table lamp was bugged. It was difficult for him to know what was happening outside, and priests beholden to the government were likely to attack his statements.

During Alexander Dubček's brief reign, Tomašek banned the Peace Priests' movement and petitioned Dubček for religious liberty. When Dubček and some of his ministers were taken to Moscow, Tomašek demanded their release. However once Gustáv Husák came to power, Tomašek disappointed many by a return to his previous caution, for he considered open opposition counterproductive. In 1977, his nomination as cardinal was announced.

That same year, he did the government a favor by dissociating the Church from an appeal for human rights known as Charter 77. Father Jozef Zvěřina, a theologian who had survived Dachau and then fifteen years in Communist prisons with his buoyancy and wit intact, sent him a scorching letter. Responding to Tomašek's expressed fear that support for Charter 77 could worsen the Church's situation, Zvěřina asked "What could make a situation already bad any worse? What could you or the Church lose?"

Zvěřina, one of the Charter 77 signatories, continued: "I implore Your Grace to try to understand in your episcopal conscience that, in our country, all means available, usually those that are evil, are used to liquidate the Church. Any concession on our part means helping in this liquidation. There is only one way: consistent, lawful resistance. There is no other way, such is the iron logic of the situation. How degrading it is that we have to defend our religious freedom irrespective of denomination, not only against the state but even against our own bishop."

Tomašek and Zvěřina were involved in a murky episode: Zvěřina wrote a letter, intended for publication in the West, denouncing persecution. Security police intercepted the letter, added Tomašek's forged signature, and forwarded the letter for publication. Then they demanded that he declare publicly he had not signed any such letter. He did so, discrediting it.

Surprisingly, the upshot of these two episodes was that Tomašek grew closer to Zvěřina and a small group of other courageous priests such as the theologian Oto Mádr; Miloslav Vlk, who was to be Tomašek's successor; and Tomáš Halík and some religious ordained clandestinely. This helped to bridge the gap between the legal and the illegal Church, which the Communists wanted to set against each other. With a radio blaring to foil bugging, these priests discussed with the cardinal in his study pastoral letters and plans. A pointer to the secrecy which prevailed is provided by Tomáš Halík, who recounted that when he proposed a ten-year pastoral-renewal program, Tomašek exclaimed: "You're almost like a deacon." Halík, who had been ordained by the future Cardinal Joachim Meisner on a visit to East Germany, wrote on a pad: "I've been a priest for years." Short Tomašek rose and embraced six-foot-two Halík. In 1988, Tomašek nominated a Committee for a Decade of Spiritual Renewal to implement Halík's proposal; most of the Czech bishops nominated after the fall of Communism were on the committee.

In 1982 the Vatican banned priests' participation in the Pacem in Terris movement. Tomašek then spoke out against the movement, the restrictions on religious activities, and the "pressure of Moscow which suffocates everything." He said he had been inspired by John Paul's "clear message in defense of human rights and, in the first place, of religious liberty."

It used to be said that, between the fourth and fifth sets of a match, Mats Wilander was the world's best tennis player. Something comparable could be said of Tomašek as a bishop between his eightieth and ninetieth years. His backbone stiffened appreciably.

Not only did he have papal backing and a worthy team of advisers but, partly through Augustin Navrotil, also found popular support. Navrotil was a farmer until Communists took his land; he then found work at the nearby railway station of Lutopecny in Moravia. His first protest was against local authorities' removal of a cross from a field. Using a home-made duplicator, in 1976 Navrotil put out a seventeen-point protest which gained 700 signatures locally and a spell in a prison psychiatric ward for him. In 1984–85 he sent copies of a new twenty-one-point protest to various government ministries, asking if it could be circulated legally. No one gave a straight answer, but again he was consigned to a prison's psychiatric ward as a paranoiac, this time for a year. He said that almost nightly fellow prisoners threatened him with death. If he was not a paranoiac on entry, he could well have been on his dismissal. But even paranoiacs, particularly in Gustáv Husák's Czechoslovakia, may have their good reasons.

Navrotil took the train to Prague and discussed his next proposed protest with a fellow Moravian who had become a protester: František Tomašek. Among its thirty-one points were the separation of Church and state, an end to the state veto on the appointment of bishops, and freedom for religious publications. With Tomašek's public backing, it was signed by over 600,000 Catholics and non-Catholics. It earned Navrotil another spell in a prison psychiatric ward. In his study in the archbishop's palace, Tomašek had a bronze sculpture of Don Quixote and Sancho Panza. Tomašek was the leader of the Czech Church but also played Sancho Panza to Navrotil when he tilted at windmills.

At least they seemed to be tilting at windmills, but a groundswell of protest was developing. In Slovakia, where Catholics were a majority, in March 1988 upwards of 15,000 attended a peace rally organized by Catholic students in the capital, Bratislava. With a brutality that indicated the regime's desperation, police beat the students and also British and Australian television crews. Twenty months later, students began the "Velvet Revolution" in Prague.

In a Mass to celebrate the canonization of St. Agnes of Bohemia in November 1989, Tomašek said, "In this decisive moment in the struggle for truth and justice, I and all the Catholic Church are on the side of the nation." Tomašek, who had entered a seminary as Czechoslovakia was established and turned its back on Vienna and Rome, had won the right to speak in the name of the nation.

He sent a message to Prague student protesters: "These people [the Communist leaders] cannot be trusted . . . we need a democratic government. I pray that you choose non-violence." He addressed Catholics specifically: "Not a single one of you may stand apart. Raise your voice . . . in unity with other citizens . . . religious rights cannot be separated from other human rights." Along with Václav Havel and Alexander Dubček, František Tomašek was acclaimed the third great figure of the resistance.

Even more than in Hungary and Czechoslovakia, John Paul's impact was felt in his homeland, where the Communists' attempt to control the Church had, instead, strengthened it. The postwar rearrangement of Polish–German–Soviet Union frontiers and the transfer of inhabitants had unwittingly produced a more Catholic and homogeneous Poland than ever before; and the Communists had begun a losing war against the Church. When in 1952 the state had claimed authority to appoint and remove bishops and priests, the Church had resisted. By 1955, 8 bishops, including Cardinal Wyszyński, and approximately 2,000 priests were imprisoned. But in 1956 social unrest brought the threat of Soviet invasion, and to calm matters the Communist leader Włdysław Gomułka recognized the Church's right to a large measure of autonomy. By the late 1970s the number of priests, about 20,000, was double that of 1945; and the Church, revitalized by resisting the repression of 1953–56, became the champion of human rights, backing workers who protested against abrupt government-imposed price increases. The Church was assuming an ever more central position in a society that was fraying.

In June 1979, for the first time Karol Wojtyła returned to Poland as John Paul II. Everywhere huge crowds gathered. At one point as he spoke in Victory Square, Warsaw, he was interrupted by applause which lasted fourteen minutes. Against the Marxist claim that religion simply expressed alienation and increased it, he asserted that religion "strengthens [man] in his natural social bonds." He demanded Polish sovereignty and made it clear that the Marxist government had not been legitimized at the polls. Poles understood his text and subtext.

Nine months after the papal visit, the consequences seemed to be that it had lifted people out of the slough of despair, convincing them that change was possible. Was this a transitory feeling? An attempt was being made to form an independent trade union, which seemed a quixotic gesture when the Party claimed to represent the workers. Surely the Party would not allow it.

Its permission was not sought. In August 1980 the whole world saw television coverage of striking workers in the Lenin Shipyard, Gdansk. Some were confessing to priests who had joined them. Huge portraits of John Paul II and the Black Madonna of Częstochowa were attached to the shipyard gates. The strike was an expression of the Solidarity movement: although its core was a trade union, it became identified with anti-Communist, antigovernment, and anti-Russian sentiment. It reached a membership of ten million, more than four times that of the Party, but this had its dangers. Its founder, Lech Wałęsa, said that seeing the crowds which had welcomed John Paul II gave him the idea of a mass movement. In Western Europe, the Church might have lost the working class; but, after forty years of Communism, Polish workers trusted the Church more than the Party and Catholic social principles more than Marxism. The Solidarity movement was not narrowly Catholic, but it was inspired and supported by John Paul

II. He welcomed its recognition by the government on November 10, 1980; and, after recovering from Ali Agca's assassination attempt of May 1981 and Cardinal Wyszyński's death that same month, he publicly deplored its outlawing on December 13, 1981.

In his Vatican audiences the pope frequently referred to the Polish situation and, for more than a year, offered a prayer to the Madonna of Częstochowa for those imprisoned under Polish martial law. During his trips to Poland in 1983 and 1987 he appealed for respect of the 1980 agreement between the government and Solidarity. If in 1983 the government hoped his visit would suggest that normalization had been achieved, he foiled this on arrival at Warsaw airport by talking of the detainees (about 1,500) who could not meet him. Moreover he received Lech Wałęsa, even though the government did not recognize him as leader of Solidarity. As he addressed crowds, they chanted "Poland is here." In 1987, although cautious changes were being made, John Paul II was welcomed by a crowd of a million Solidarity supporters in Gdansk, the city which gave birth to the movement. He reiterated the right of workers to form trade unions. His public appeals for workers' rights must be set in the context of the Polish Church's unceasing efforts to avoid providing any excuse for Soviet intervention or violence between Poles. The aim was not to smash the social system but to transform it.

Fortunately, President Wojciech Jaruzelski came to recognize that economic survival required an agreement with Solidarity. Negotiations lasted from February to April 1989; in June that year the first partially free elections were held and Solidarity-backed candidates won overwhelmingly. Soviet intervention would have been the only way to block Poland's choice, but Gorbachev's rejection of the Brezhnev Doctrine of limited sovereignty had ruled that out. It was the beginning of the end for Communism in much of Central and Eastern Europe.

Chapter 7

Millennium in Moscow

Because Cardinal Stefan Wyszyński was diffident about Vatican *Ostpolitik* and its chief negotiator, Agostino Casaroli, some were surprised when John Paul II, who had profound respect for Wyszyński, made Casaroli his Secretary of State in April 1979. But it was also said that Wyszyński himself had advised the pope to choose Casaroli, partly on the grounds that "the devil you know . . ."

Casaroli, who had begun working in the Secretariat of State just before World War II, represented the continuity of Vatican diplomacy. Because relations with Italy would always be delicate, it was sensible to have an Italian as number two to balance a Polish pope. As it turned out, Casaroli's patience and subtlety nicely offset John Paul's bolder style. This was evident in his dealings with the Soviet Foreign Minister Andrei Gromyko. After the visit of Khrushchev's son-in-law, Aleksei Adjubei, to John XXIII on March 7, 1963, a series of Soviet leaders came to the Vatican. When Nikolai Podgorny, President of the Supreme Soviet, visited Paul VI on January 30, 1967, the pope mentioned the problems of the Catholic Church in the Soviet Union. "We'll see," said Podgorny; "they could be discussed."

On each of Gromyko's visits, Paul VI raised the question of religious rights, but the foreign minister turned a deaf ear, saying it was not in his competency. Cardinal Casaroli has recounted that it was like running up against a rubber wall, adding that on one occasion Gromyko, pretending not to understand, turned to the Soviet ambassador and said "Religious questions? But we have good relations with our Patriarch!" In default of answers to his queries, Paul VI had to be satisfied with having raised the question.

John Paul, however, crashed through the rubber wall: Gromyko tried the "you've been badly informed" response when John Paul mentioned religious problems, but the pope told him the information was accurate and he awaited solutions. The Soviets did not appreciate this directness any more than did the Russian Orthodox appreciate his summoning in Rome, in November–December 1980, a synod of the Ukrainian Catholic Church, which they had absorbed in 1946.

Moreover the Polish situation was tense. In line with criticism made by the Communist Party ideologue Mikhail Suslov, the Soviet press attacked John Paul as a "political pope." The nadir of John Paul II–Kremlin relations was August 26, 1984, when the pope publicly denounced a Soviet veto of a trip by Cardinal Casaroli to Lithuania. But Mikhail Gorbachev, who became the Soviet leader in 1985, recognized the need for changes in Soviet Bloc countries and the possibility that the Church would ensure that they took place in Poland without violence.

As late as November 1986 Gorbachev had called for an "energetic and implacable struggle" against religion and the reinforcement of atheistic propaganda (as he spoke in Tashkent, these words may have been inspired mainly by fear of Islamic fundamentalism). His book *Perestroika* showed little interest in religion, but at a certain point he began to make overtures to the Russian Orthodox Church, which had the allegiance of an estimated 50 million faithful, and to praise religion because it could offset pervasive apathy. Reportedly, Gorbachev's grandparents, like other peasants, rather than destroy their icons as the atheists had demanded simply covered them with portraits of Lenin and Stalin.

Metaphorically speaking, Gorbachev had removed Stalin's portrait and was content with the icon underneath, as indicated in April 1988, when he cordially received Patriarch Pimen of Moscow with other Orthodox bishops and approved the celebration of Prince Vladimir's conversion to Christianity in 988. Vladimir's conversion had resulted in the conversion of all the inhabitants of the Rus of Kiev, which, Gorbachev acknowledged, marked an entry to European civilization. The Russian Orthodox Church invited the Vatican to send a delegation of cardinals to the millennium celebrations. Did it ever! The largest delegation despatched anywhere at any time—nine cardinals—was nominated. It was headed by Cardinal Casaroli and included Johannes Willebrands, president of the Secretariat for Christian Unity, who had long been responsible for the Vatican's relations with the Russian Orthodox Church.

The cardinals found Moscow in June sweltering under a sun hotter than Rome's: it was the hottest summer in over a century. Many Muscovites wore crosses and millennium badges; radio and television appealed for funds to rebuild churches; for the occasion, the thirteenth-century Danilov Monastery complex had been refurbished and returned to the Orthodox as their "Vatican"; the museums of atheism and religion began to downplay the first term in favor of the second. Scores of "prisoners of conscience" had been released. Guides tried hard: one explained that a copy of Andrei Rublev's fifteenth-century icon "The Trinity" represented the unity of Russia, Ukraine, and Belarus, then gave as an alternative explanation that it was an illustration of the "phrase of our immortal writer Leo Tolstoy: whenever two or three gather together in my name, I am among them." There was also a story of two seventy-year-old women who compared notes: they agreed that all their lives they had been told that God did not exist, but recently the press, radio, and television spoke of God all the time. One asked: "Where did he spring from?"

The millennium had brought Christianity back to the center of the Soviet scene, but it had been present even earlier if one cared to look. In the Kremlin itself the most beautiful square consisted of four churches, which had been transformed into museums, and a palace, one of the rare historic civic buildings in a city whose mainly wooden constructions had repeatedly been destroyed by fire. When Soviet citizens looked back beyond 1917 in any city except Leningrad, they saw little else but evidence of the historical importance of religion. For contemporary buildings, in Moscow they had twelve ugly Stalinist towers, massive apartment buildings, and glass-cube hotels. For beauty, they still had only churches.

Millennium guests visited the Trinity–St. Sergius Monastery complex at Zagorsk, forty-five miles north of Moscow, which had withstood Mongol and Polish forces as well as seventy years of atheism. After an empty countryside with occasional nondescript buildings, its many churches' onion domes were dazzling silver against a blue sky.

A Russian journalist, Vitali Vitaliev, has revealed that from the early 1950s one of Zagorsk's churches was used for nuclear research. As there was little protection against radiation, none of those who worked there (including Vitaliev's father) lived to the age of sixty. "What a terrible sacrilege," wrote Vitaliev, "to use churches (even if they were former ones) for production of the devil's weapon. No other social system must have been capable of such a blasphemy."

But the visitors to the Trinity–St. Sergius Monastery did not know this. They saw only bearded priests offering bread and salt, the traditional symbols of welcome, and heard countless bells pealing and rippling at different tempos; although bell-ringing had been banned for years, the skills had survived. It seemed they were celebrating the resurrection of Christianity. The many churches and monasteries were of varying pastel colors, and flowers bloomed. It created a brilliant, joyous impression after the drab workers' paradise.

Near the tomb of St. Sergius, the monastery's founder, people prayed in candlelit penumbra before a copy of Rublev's icon "The Trinity": they were already halfway to heaven, to the real, spiritual world that opened out to them from the icon. In an adjoining building, a local council of the Russian Orthodox Church was canonizing the monk Rublev and eight others: it was the first time since the Revolution that a local council had canonized saints. For the Russian Orthodox Church the four-day council, attended by representatives of Orthodox and other churches from all over the world, was the millennium's main event.

It seemed a triumph, but there were shadows. One was cast by people such as Father Gleb Jakunin who had suffered prison for their faith and questioned even the legitimacy of the Russian Orthodox hierarchy. Formerly they had accused it of collusion with the regime, but now, somewhat paradoxically, they complained it was not sufficiently responsive to *perestroika* and the people's spiritual hunger.

The second shadow on Russian Orthodoxy's sunlit celebrations was a group of two bishops, three priests, and three laymen who came from West Ukraine to Moscow that June. They were of the Ukrainian Catholic Church, which had been taken over by the Russian Orthodox in 1946. For the Orthodox these members of a supposedly extinct church were "ghosts" who threatened to spoil the feast. For the cardinals from Rome they were persecuted brethren but also a potential embarrassment during this unique opportunity to improve relations with the Orthodox and, in the case of Casaroli, to get on talking terms with Gorbachev.

Ukrainian Catholics had wanted to boycott Orthodox celebrations of the millennium and were deeply offended when they heard that a Vatican delegation was to attend, shake hands, and celebrate the liturgy with their persecutors. One of the delegation from Ukraine, Father Mykhaylo Havryliv, who had been an Orthodox priest, said in Moscow that the

"Russian Orthodox is a state Church whereas the Ukrainian Catholic Church is a people's Church." The eight Ukrainian Catholics lodged with a lawyer friend. Soviet officials blocked their access to Cardinal Casaroli in the Sovietskaya Hotel, but they got a note to him and were allowed to enter. At 5 P.M. on Friday, June 10, the Ukrainians began a ninety-minute meeting with Cardinal Willebrands and his assistant, an American Jesuit, Father John Long. Bishop Filymon Korchaba, speaking in Ukrainian with an interpreter from the patriarchate, described the situation of the still semiclandestine Church in West Ukraine. The Ukrainians hoped that Casaroli, who arrived towards the end of the meeting, would put their case to Gorbachev.

But there had been no indication that Casaroli would be received by Gorbachev, despite an assurance given by the Soviet ambassador in Rome before Casaroli's departure. For Casaroli it was the end of his twenty-five year Long March to the heart of the empire. With him, when he stepped off the Aeroflot jet at Moscow airport, he brought the First Epistle to the Soviets: a handwritten letter for Gorbachev from John Paul II which outlined the case for religious liberty and, in a substantial appendix, detailed the situation of Catholics in various Soviet republics.

At least Casaroli was doing better than Achille Ratti, the future Pius XI, had done when he was nuncio in Warsaw: in September 1918 Ratti had been furnished with a letter from Benedict XV's Secretary of State, which he was to consign in Moscow to Georgy Vasilevic Cicerin, People's Commissar for Foreign Affairs. But despite phone calls to Lenin from Warsaw, Ratti was not allowed to enter Russia. Casaroli, however, had taken a direct Rome-Moscow flight. Alceste Santini, the Vatican correspondent of the Italian Communist daily *L'Unità,* was on Casaroli's flight and interviewed him. Other journalists covering the millennium celebrations doubted whether the Casaroli–*L'Unità* correspondent meeting

was accidental. The outcome was a prominent article high-
lighting the fact that Casaroli was bearing a papal letter
for Gorbachev. It was presumed that Casaroli had used
L'Unità, one of the few Western papers available in Moscow,
to remind Soviet authorities of his aims. However, there was
no hint that they had noticed Casaroli's intentions when, on
Saturday, June 11, four days before he was to return to Rome,
he and other millennium participants were invited by Andrei
Gromyko to the yellow Presidium building near the Kremlin's
Spassky Gate.

The high-ceilinged, windowless chamber where the meeting took place was white and aseptic. Gromyko, who
presided seated at a dais, was a peerless survivor, at the end
of the road but at the top of the heap. He was head of state
although, with his crooked mouth, grey hair, and neutral manner, he still seemed merely a diligent bureaucrat. Alongside
Gromyko was white-bearded Patriarch Pimen, who reportedly
was in poor health, but his voice was strong when he
addressed the head of state as "Andrei Andreievich."

Gromyko occasionally cupped his hand behind his ear to
hear questions from the guests in their terraced seats: Muftis,
Shintoists, cardinals, and others raised their hands to attract
attention like students in a lecture hall. He deftly handled the
questions, then gave the floor to Casaroli, whom he knew
from meetings in the Vatican and at the United Nations headquarters. Casaroli spoke of the Church's work for peace and
human rights, then pointed out that there had never been so
many cardinals (some were seated beside him) in the Third
Rome. (Moscow claimed this label in the sixteenth century,
when it became the headquarters of the Russian Orthodox
Church. When Constantinople was established by Emperor
Constantine in the fourth century, it had arrogated the title
"the Second Rome"; Moscow saw itself as the third and last
Rome). It was a tribute, Casaroli continued, to the Russian
Orthodox Church and the USSR's community of peoples. He

was followed by Cardinal Willebrands, who unexpectedly asked whether believers would be consulted during the preparation of a new religious law. Gromyko said it would be logical to know the views of the Churches; he did not say in so many words that they would be consulted.

After this unprecedented meeting, drinks were offered in the adjoining hall. Casaroli parried questions about the undelivered papal letter, but even he was perplexed. It was unfortunate that Foreign Minister Eduard Shevardnadze, who might have helped, was in New York. On the outskirts of the group around Casaroli, wearing a grey suit and blue tie, was a handsome, bespectacled man with tousled, greying hair. He smiled at everyone but spoke to no one until he grasped Casaroli's hand, saying, "I'm Leonardo Boff." Even quick-witted Casaroli seemed wrong-footed momentarily, perhaps mindful that the Brazilian liberation theologian's recent starry-eyed praise of the Soviet system implied that there was no need for improvement in believers' conditions.

Casaroli was in a quandary. He was lodged in the hotel reserved for government guests rather than in that which the patriarchate had reserved for the other cardinals and religious figures. The Soviet authorities had treated him as the Vatican prime minister, but he was stalled over the papal letter. He considered consigning it to Gromyko, who was head of state, or to the Minister for Religion, whom he was to meet the following day; but in either case it would be an admission of failure.

As the guests went towards a reception in the Kremlin's St. George's Hall, Casaroli sought help from Alceste Santini of *L'Unità,* who sometimes handled diplomatic tasks in the Vatican for Eastern countries as well as his journalistic tasks. Casaroli asked Santini if he could discover the Soviet authorities' intentions. In St. George's Hall, Santini immediately put the question to a Soviet historian friend, Andrei Kowalsky, who was a consultant to Gorbachev. At another reception at the Prague Restaurant the following afternoon, Kowalsky confirmed the Gorbachev meeting. Santini took a taxi to the Sovietskaya Hotel to tell Casaroli the welcome news that he would be received at noon on the following day. It seems that what Casaroli called "the sand in the machinery" was caused by those who maintained Gorbachev should not give importance to a Vatican representative. Eduard Shevardnadze had returned and had helped remove the sand.

Not only did Gorbachev accept John Paul's letter, but he talked with Casaroli for a full ninety minutes. On his return to the Sovietskaya Hotel, Casaroli was jubilant. "Gorbachev and I were frank and the atmosphere cordial," said Casaroli, which meant they had crossed swords but it had not been a fight to the death. "This enabled us to say things that in other circumstances might have been unpleasant. It's the first time that Soviet authorities have accepted outside representations about the rights of some of their citizens. It's a step, a first step towards what I hope will become regular contacts."

A Russian Orthodox bishop was present, as was Cardinal Roger Etchegaray, president of the Vatican Council for Justice and Peace, who began to talk enthusiastically about the Catholic Church's interest in its sister Church's millennium. Presumably, he feared that the Orthodox prelate would conclude the cardinals had come not for the millennium but, instead, to establish ties with the Kremlin; of course they had both aims. As Etchegaray's rapid French spilled out, Casaroli nodded occasionally and smiled, but it could have been in satisfaction at the twenty-five years of little steps that had brought him to Moscow. Now it could be downhill all the way: a John Paul II–Gorbachev meeting, exchange of diplomatic representatives, and further ahead perhaps even a papal trip to Moscow.

By the time John Paul and Mikhail Gorbachev met in the Vatican on December 1, 1989, the Berlin Wall had fallen. Only a few days before, Václav Havel, the playwright–Charter 77 signatory who had become president of Czechoslovakia, had invited John Paul there. It had been prophesied that the conquering Cossacks' horses would drink from the fountains in St. Peter's Square, but now a popemobile crossing Red Square seemed more likely. In fact, Gorbachev invited John Paul to the Soviet Union, but the pope asked first that a new, more equitable religious law be introduced and that the Ukrainian Catholic Church be recognized, as it subsequently was. An exchange of diplomatic representatives was a further consequence of the meeting.

Gorbachev professed to be delighted to find a pope who was Slav, while John Paul welcomed *perestroika* in no uncertain terms. He was grateful for the removal of the Soviet military threat and believed in Gorbachev's good intentions. The problem was that John Paul liked Gorbachev more than did his own people. The last politician given similar praise as a man of providence, remarked the pensioned-off Italian Cardinal Silvio Oddi, was Benito Mussolini.

In Rome, Gorbachev not only spoke of believers having a right to follow their consciences but of religion contributing to social renovation. His viewpoint, welcomed by the Vatican, was expressed also by other Soviet officials at international conferences. Previously the Soviet Union's relations with the Holy See were based on the coincidence of views on issues such as peace, disarmament, and international conflicts; but they could be closer if the Soviets assessed religion itself positively.

This could account for Gorbachev's invitation to the pope as well as a desire for John Paul II's support of *perestroika:* in the international sphere, the Catholic Church carried more weight than the Russian Orthodox Church, which he had courted. John Paul had made no secret of his desire to visit Moscow, nor did he underestimate its importance. "When I go to the Soviet Union," he had said while flying over Africa four years before, "it will be a great turning point in the history of Christianity and of the world."

But the Soviet Union was disbanded before John Paul II arrived there, and the Vatican hurriedly sought contact with

Boris Yeltsin. The Vatican "Minister for Foreign Affairs," Jean-Louis Tauran, met him in Moscow in September 1991. Yeltsin may have acquired a certain sympathy for Catholicism when a Catholic radio station provided the equipment which enabled him to communicate with the populace during the attempted 1991 coup. But his closest links, of course, were with the Orthodox Church, into which he had been baptized. Patriarch Alexy supported Yeltsin at the time of the coup and tried, unsuccessfully, to mediate in the 1993 Yeltsin-parliament clash.

In their first meeting in the Vatican on December 20, 1992, John Paul was feeling his way with Yeltsin, who guaranteed that all Russian citizens would enjoy full religious rights. One effect of the disintegration of the Soviet Union is that Moscow now rules a territory in which the proportion of Catholics is lower than before and that of the Orthodox higher. Orthodox antipapal sentiments were particularly strong at the time of Yeltsin's papal audience. He did not invite John Paul to Moscow and, after the audience, said that Gorbachev had already done this. It was hardly time for a papal trip there; and, in any case, there must be a limit to the Russians' capacity for historic turning points.

Chapter 8

A Vision of Europe

Without hesitation John Paul II described the changes in Central and Eastern Europe as "the result of the intervention of God, who directs the course of history towards its eschatological goal 'to unite all things in Christ.'" John Paul furnished a vivid, as yet unfinished story of God's victory over evil in which Karol Wojtyła, while calling himself evangelically "a useless servant," has a key role. Another participant in this story is Our Lady of Fatima.

John Paul stressed the influence of prayer and suffering on the changes in Central and Eastern Europe. What of the prayers for the conversion of Russia said for decades at the end of Mass by hundreds of millions of Catholics? What of Our Lady of Fatima? In 1917, shortly after the Russian Revolution, three young Portuguese shepherds saw a figure in the sky who, among other things, asked all bishops to consecrate the world to the Virgin Mary to bring about the conversion of Russia. (One of the shepherds, Lucia, who had never heard of "Russia," is said to have thought it was a girl's name.) If the consecration to the Virgin Mary took place, there would be peace; if the message was ignored, Russia would spread its errors throughout the world, there would be wars and persecution, and the pope would suffer greatly.

Although urgent, the message was not disclosed until 1942, which led some to claim it was a later addition. It is the second secret of Fatima (the first concerned the early death of two of the three shepherds, which punctually took

109

place). The world has been consecrated to the Virgin Mary several times since, most recently by John Paul II in 1984. But for one reason or another, some Fatima enthusiasts have not been satisfied—for instance, they claim that, for fear of offending Russia, John Paul did not mention it specifically, or at least audibly, during the consecration. The Vatican has not disclosed the third secret of Fatima, written down in 1957 by the sole surviving shepherd, Lucia, who became a nun; it is rumored to be apocalyptic.

Phenomena such Fatima do not add anything to revelation. They are a call to conversion that can inspire fervor but also cranks. Some Fatima-inspired groups set other Catholics' teeth on edge; but John Paul II is devoted to Our Lady of Fatima, and he believes that she saved him from death when Ali Agca tried to assassinate him and also that she "guided people to freedom."

The assassination attempt took place on May 13, 1981, the sixty-fourth anniversary of the first vision in Fatima. On the first anniversary of the attack, John Paul went to Fatima to thank the Virgin for her help; and he returned in May 1991 to reaffirm his gratitude: "on May 13, 1981, I felt your helpful presence beside me." For the occasion, the bullet removed from his abdomen was inserted in the pearl- and precious stone-encrusted golden crown of the Virgin's statue which was carried in procession.

John Paul II gave the impression that since the beginning of his reign he had been challenging God to give a sign so that people might believe. He seemed to see the reversal of fortunes in Central and Eastern Europe as such a sign and wanted to make the purblind recognize it through striking gestures such as linking the sufferings of Christians in Communist Europe with his own from Ali Agca's bullet. But those who expected him to announce an apocalyptic future in Fatima were disappointed. "From Fatima," said John Paul II, "a consoling light full of hope seems to illuminate the facts of the end of this second millennium. The events of late 1989 and early 1990 were a historic turning point in this difficult twentieth century. With the end of the division between two blocs based on opposed ideological and socio-economic principles, nations have a new prospect." He spoke of a dawn for humanity and for the Church.

Instead of the anticipated warnings against imminent death and destruction, he pointed towards the new Jerusalem. John Paul II is not apocalyptic but millennarian in the sense that, as his apostolic letter *Tertio millennio adveniente* showed, he expects the third millennium to be a new phase in human history. Not only does he use the third millennium as a horizon to spur Christians to a new evangelization, but he seems to believe that millennia have a special significance—he has pointed out that the substantial changes in Poland and the Soviet Union followed closely on the celebrations, in 1968 and 1988 respectively, of the millennia of Christianity in those countries. (As the end of the first millennium coincided roughly with the acceptance of Christianity in the Rus of Kiev, in Poland, and in Hungary, Central and Eastern European Christians tend to look to the end of the millennium with hope whereas Westerners tend to view it with foreboding.)

For John Paul, Fatima and sensible, optimistic, socio-political comments are compatible. He addressed similar percipient analyses to the Madonna of Jasna Góra shrine in Częstochowa. He sees the changes in Central and Eastern Europe, like his election, as part of a providential design. Providence had chosen him as pope, John Paul said in Poland in June 1979, "to proclaim the spiritual unity of Christian Europe." A corollary of Europe's spiritual unity was that its division sanctioned at Yalta could not be justified. Further, John Paul said that perhaps the first Slav to be bishop of Rome had been elected so that "the words and languages which still sound strange in the Church used to Romance, Germanic, Celtic, and Anglo-Saxon sounds should be understood."

In other words, John Paul was to be the voice of the Slavs, a new Cyril or Methodius, the brothers who were the subject of his 1985 encyclical *Slavorum Apostoli.* John Paul also made them copatrons of Europe with St. Benedict—not patrons of Eastern Europe, note, but of Europe as a whole, together with the founder of Western monasticism nominated by Paul VI as patron of Europe. Their major achievement was to create the Slavonic alphabet and to use it to evangelize Slavs, which means that Slavic culture and identity have a Christian basis. Even today, as John Paul wrote in *Slavorum Apostoli,* Old Slavonic "is the language used in the Byzantine liturgy of the Slavonic Eastern Churches of the Rite of Constantinople, both Catholic and Orthodox, in Eastern and Southern Europe, as well as in various countries of Western Europe. It is also used in the Roman liturgy of the Catholics of Croatia."

Cyril and Methodius were sons of Leo, a Byzantine government official in Greek-speaking Salonica. Cyril, the youngest of Leo's seven children, was born in 827 about twelve years after Methodius. Revealing notable memory and linguistic skills, he studied in the best college of the Byzantine capital, Constantinople. After a period as librarian-secretary to the patriarch of Constantinople, he taught philosophy.

Around 860, the two brothers were members of an imperial delegation which went to negotiate with Muslims. After that, probably because of uncongenial political developments, Cyril withdrew to a monastery run by his brother, who had had legal training and had also served in the public administration. Later, Cyril was appointed to another imperial delegation to the Khazari, converts to Judaism who lived in the Caucasus. There Cyril located what he believed were the bones of St. Clement, the third successor of St. Peter, who was thought to have been exiled to the Crimea.

On return to Constantinople, Cyril wanted to rest but was entrusted with his last and greatest mission: Rostislav, Slav prince of Moravia, requested missionaries for his domain which included parts of today's Czech Republic, Slovakia, Hungary, and the former Yugoslavia. Missionaries from Germanic-speaking lands, many of them Irish and Scots, had already brought Christianity to Rostislav's domains; but he wanted to free himself from Germanic influence. He had requested missionaries from Rome but, receiving no response, had turned to Constantinople, asking also for a code of civil law.

The Byzantine Empire's culture was Greek, and it hellenized its Slav subjects as quickly as possible; but since Moravia was outside the empire Greek could not be imposed. Nevertheless it was thought worthwhile to send missionaries to extend Byzantine influence at the expense of the Germans.

There had been many Slavs in Salonica, so Cyril and Methodius were familiar with the spoken language. But it did not have an alphabet and thus could not be written. In preparation for his mission, Cyril returned to a monastery and devised a thirty-nine letter alphabet based mainly on Greek letters, to which he added some signs to make it faithful to Slavic sounds (this alphabet influenced a later one called "Cyrillic" after the missionary). He then translated the Old and New Testaments and liturgical books into Slavonic. His evangelization kit was ready.

In about 862, Cyril, Methodius, and a half dozen other missionaries set out for Moravia. When they presented the scriptures in Slavonic they were enthusiastically received by all but the Germanic missionaries, who claimed the Gospel could be preached and the Mass celebrated only in Latin, Greek, or Hebrew, the languages in the inscription on Jesus' cross. Cyril and Methodius went to Rome in 867 to seek approval for the Slav liturgy. They had a persuasive argument: they brought with them what were believed to be St. Clement's remains. Pope Hadrian II upheld their use of Slavonic in the Mass (they were probably using the Latin rather than the Eastern rite). Cyril, who became a monk in his last years, died in Rome in 869 and was buried in the church of St. Clement; Methodius returned to Moravia as archbishop and papal legate for all Slavs.

But Methodius was imprisoned in Bavaria for three years and treated harshly by its bishops. Pope John VII wrote to one of them: "You have tortured [Methodius], leaving him in the open for a long time exposed to the cold and rain . . . You even wanted to whip him in front of the episcopal conference." Germanic missionaries eventually regained control in Moravia, and in 885 the approximately 200 priests faithful to the deceased Methodius were driven out. A large number were welcomed by the Bulgarian King Boris, who had converted to Christianity twenty years earlier. These spiritual sons of Cyril and Methodius played an important role in establishing Christianity in Bulgaria, particularly by opening schools there. In turn, Bulgarian Christianity played a part in the establishment of Christianity in Kiev. Other priests faithful to Methodius settled in eastern Poland.

The use of Slavonic for evangelization and liturgy, John Paul has claimed, transformed it into a literary language that helped shape cultures and national identities. He has also underlined that, although Cyril and Methodius set out from Constantinople, this was before the split with Rome; and they appealed to Rome's authority. He saw this as evidence that the great spiritual traditions of East and West can be complementary rather than conflicting; they are branches of the one Church, two lungs which Europe needs to breathe.

"Cyril and Methodius," he affirmed in *Slavorum Apostoli,* "are as it were the connecting links or spiritual bridge between the Eastern and Western traditions, which both came together in the one great tradition of the universal Church. For us they are the champions and also the patrons of the ecumenical endeavors of the Sister Churches of East and West for the rediscovery through prayer and dialogue of visible unity in perfect and total communion, 'the unity which,' as I [have] said . . . 'is neither absorption nor fusion.'"

John Paul's understanding of Cyril and Methodius is crucial to his vision of Europe, which is civil as well as religious: "Cyril and Methodius made a decisive contribution to the building of Europe not only in Christian religious communion but also to its civil and cultural union. Not even today does there exist any other way of overcoming tensions and repairing the divisions and antagonisms both in Europe and the world which threaten to cause a frightful destruction of lives and values. Being Christians in our day means being builders of communion in the Church and in society."

The connections between early Christian Kiev and Rome have been underlined by John Paul. And he is mindful that Christianity came to Poland "by the Slav route" through St. Adalbert, who was archbishop of Prague. He made a point of announcing the special synod for Europe, held in 1991, at the tomb of St. Methodius in Velehrad, Moravia.

But John Paul has underplayed the fact that the Slavs are unique among European people for receiving their Christianity through two such distinct rites. Broadly speaking, the Western Slavs (Poles, Czechs, and Slovaks) and the Southern Slavs (Croats and Slovenes, not the Serbs) are Latin-rite and the remainder Eastern-rite. All credit to John Paul II, a Latin-rite Slav, who has paid generous tribute to Eastern-rite Slavs. But the rites question has exacerbated divisions, as seen, for instance, in the nationalist-religious tensions between Eastern-rite Ukrainian Catholics and Latin-rite Polish Catholics in eastern Poland. The twin tradition implies enriching diversity but also division. If Byzantine influence had persisted until today on a large scale, rather than in small areas of southern Italy with an Eastern-rite liturgy and customs, it would probably have augmented contrasts between northern and southern Italy.

Although he talks out of his condition as a Pole and Slav, John Paul has a vision of Europe as a whole. He maintains that Europe must recall where it comes from to find where it should go, but he does not want to restore medieval Christendom. He affirms pluralism and condemns Christians' nostalgia for "an often idealized past."

"Medieval Latin Christianity," he said before the European parliament in Strasbourg in October 1988 ". . . did not avoid the integralist temptation to exclude from the temporal community those who did not profess the true faith. Religious integralism, which did not distinguish between the sphere of faith and that of social life, as still occurs today in some countries, appears incompatible with the European spirit as shaped by the Christian message."

John Paul envisages a Europe of many faiths and none in which Christians make their voice heard in the public sphere. "Europe is a significant example of the spiritual fecundity of Christianity which cannot be relegated to the private sphere," he said in Strasbourg. "It is my duty to underline that if the continent's religious and Christian basis is marginalized as inspiration for ethics and as a social influence, it will not only negate all Europe's heritage but a future worthy of European man—both believers and non-believers—will be compromised." He was to repeat the message on his visit to Germany in July 1996, underlining that it did not imply "restoring a long-dead past."

His encyclical *Centesimus annus* was not only a commemoration of Leo XIII's *Rerum novarum* but a response to the events of 1989. It celebrated the collapse of European Communism but warned also about capitalism's shortcomings. Concerned to ensure the priority of labor over capital, John Paul recommended a market economy regulated by a state which protects workers. After noting that in the 1980s dictatorial and oppressive regimes fell in Latin America, Africa, and Asia, he pointed out that European Communism was defeated by "peaceful protests, using only the weapons of truth and justice."

He acknowledged that another factor in its fall was the inefficiency of the economic system, which "is not to be considered simply as a technical problem but rather a consequence of the violation of the human right to private initiative, to ownership of property, and to freedom in the economic sector." He mentioned also the denial of the human "cultural and national dimension" under Communism.

But the basic cause of the events of 1989, claimed John Paul, was "the spiritual void brought about by atheism," which "deprived the younger generation of a sense of direction and in many cases led them, in the irrepressible search for personal identity and for the meaning of life, to discover the religious roots of their national culture . . . Marxism had promised to uproot the need for God from the human heart but the results have shown that this is not possible without throwing the heart into turmoil." The events of 1989, he claimed, had disproved those who recommend "an impossible compromise between Marxism and Christianity" but reaffirmed "an authentic theology of human liberation."

But after liberation from Communism which had oppressed them, Orthodox and Catholics did not embrace. John Paul wanted Europe to breathe, as he said, "with its two lungs," to harmonize its Latin-Western with its Byzantine-Eastern traditions. Instead, between Orthodox and Catholics old enmities reemerged in acrimonious disputes. As a result, John Paul's vision of Europe was contradicted by those who were to be its foundation: many of them were at each other's throats.

Tomáš Halík, who studied for the priesthood and was ordained in secret, is a leader in helping the Czech Church adjust to post-Communist freedom.

A painting of the Bulgarian Eugheni Bossilkov (1900–52), C.P., bishop
of Nikopol, the first Catholic bishop–victim of Communism after
World War II whose beatification was approved.

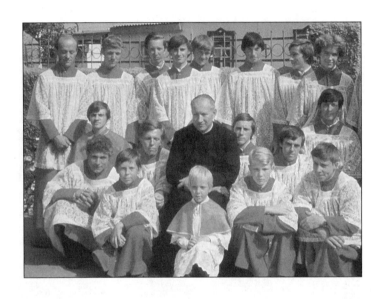

Albinas Dumbliauskas, S.J., who served in Lithuania, Siberia, and Kazakhstan, often covered his priestly ministry by working as an ambulance driver.

Otto Messmer, S.J., with young Catholics in Akmola, Kazakhstan.

Aleksandr Ogorodnikov, who founded a Christian study circle in Moscow in 1974, later suffered hunger and cold in a labor camp, where, he has written, "any manifestation of such Christian impulses as mercy, compassion, defense of the persecuted, and love" was forbidden. He survived to celebrate his wedding in a traditional Orthodox ceremony.

Sigitas Tamkevičius, S.J., displays the typewriter with changeable type he used to foil K.G.B. agents as he published the *Chronicle of the Catholic Church in Lithuania;* he became archbishop of Kaunas, Lithuania, in May 1996. (*Company, A Jesuit Magazine/*James Vorwoldt, S.J.)

Sister Nijolė Sadūnaitė and Father Alfonsas Svarinskas worked for human rights in Lithuania and nonviolently challenged the regime; both were arrested and convicted for their activities. (Aid to the Church in Need)

In Brest, Belarus, Father Kazimierz Swiatek was a prisoner of the K.G.B., of the German army, and of the Russian army; in 1990 at the age of seventy-six he was made archbishop of Minsk-Mohilev and in November 1994 was made a cardinal. (J. C. Gadmer/CIRIC)

On November 2, 1990, All Souls Day, Father Simon Jubani celebrated the
first public mass in decades at a cemetery in Shkodër, Albania.

Cardinal Jozef Beran of Prague, Czechoslovakia, was imprisoned by both the Nazis and the Communists.

As a pseudonym for the books he wrote during the Communist era, Cardinal Ján Chryzostom Korec of Nitra, Slovakia, used "a worker in overalls," an accurate description. (J. C. Gadmer/CIRIC)

When Alojzije Stepinac of Zagreb was named a cardinal by Pope Pius
XII, the Yugoslavian government broke off diplomatic relations with the
Vatican. (KNA-Bild)

The trial of Cardinal József Mindszenty in 1948 drew worldwide
attention to Communist persecution of the Church. (KNA-Bild)

František Tomašek headed the Church in Prague from 1963 to 1991; initially he was cautious in dealing with the Communist regime but towards the end became an outspoken opponent.

John Paul II drew crowds throughout his first visit to Poland as pope in 1979.

15.05.1977

Communist authorities built Nowa Huta as a new, churchless industrial
city near Cracow; from a house-church in the early 1950s the Christian
community grew until authorities allowed construction of a large church,
which Cardinal Karol Wojtyła dedicated in May 1977.

In 1978 Mykhaylo Havryliv, an Orthodox priest, became a Ukrainian-rite
Catholic; as a punishment for publishing a book about his decision he was
appointed to a cleanup crew in Chernobyl after the nuclear boildown.
(Aid to the Church in Need)

In Lviv and in Rome, Cardinal Josyf Slipyj was a tireless campaigner for the rights of Ukrainian Catholics.

For decades Volodymyr Sterniuk, C.SS.R., a clandestine bishop in Lviv, Ukraine, worked as a bookkeeper, librarian, and forestry guard, all the while carrying on his priestly ministry.

At Easter liturgy in St. George Cathedral, Lviv, are Metropolitan Maxim Hermajuk, Cardinal Myroslav Lubachivsky, and Metropolitan Volodymyr Sterniuk. (Aid to the Church in Need)

In 1990 Pope John Paul II met for the first time with the bishops of
Ukraine. (KNA-Bild)

Cardinal Myroslav Lubachivsky returned to Lviv, Ukraine, at Easter 1991. (Aid to the Church in Need)

Father Werenfried van Straaten (r.) meets with Russian Patriarch Alexy II;
Father van Straaten, a Dutch Norbertine who helped Germans after World
War II and then extended aid to Catholics under Communist regimes
through the Aid to the Church in Need organization, which he founded,
by 1993 considered reconciliation between Catholics and Orthodox as his
greatest challenge. (Andrzej Polec)

Archbishop Tadeusz Kondrusiewicz graduated as a hydraulic engineer
but became Apostolic Administrator for the European Part of Russia.
(Markus Maria Plur)

Bishop Joseph Werth, S.J., is the Apostolic Administrator of Siberia; he
resides in Novosibirsk. (*Company, A Jesuit Magazine*)

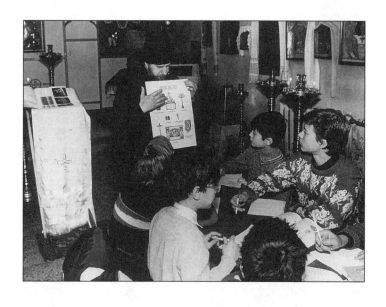

Religious instruction is a recent innovation in this Russian Orthodox
parish. (Andrzej Polec)

The Communists built a swimming pool in a confiscated Lutheran church
in St. Petersburg, installing diving boards in what had been the sanctuary.
(Andrzej Polec)

In September 1978 Miloslav Vlk lost his state license for priestly ministry; his crime was teaching children catechism. He worked in a nail-and-screw factory and later as a window cleaner; he also continued secret priestly ministry. He is now cardinal–archbishop of Prague.

A section of the Berlin Wall stands in the Vatican Gardens with the words
of Pope John Paul II nearby: "Be not afraid. Open your doors to Christ,
throw them wide open to his salvific dominion, open state borders and
political and economic systems. Be not afraid." (*L'Osservatore Romano*)

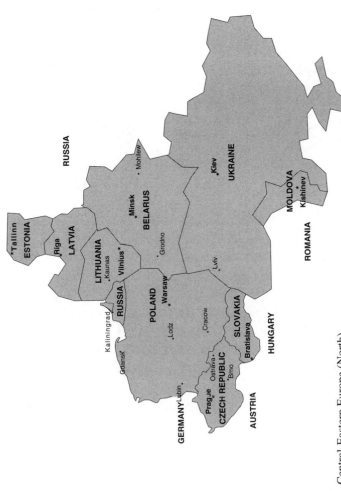

Central-Eastern Europe (North)

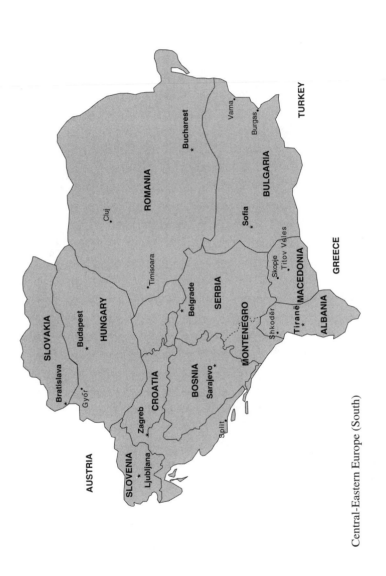

Central-Eastern Europe (South)

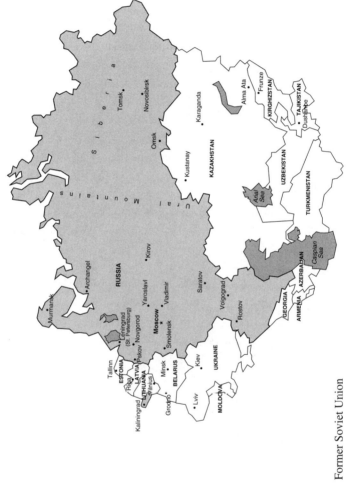

Former Soviet Union

Chapter 9

Never the Twain
Shall Meet?

Traveler, if you go to Rome, tell them that we have
remained faithful.
An emendation of an inscription on a monument to
the heroes of Thermopylae

Prince Vladimir, as the story is told, at the end of the tenth
century sent envoys to assess the most suitable religion to
adopt now that he wanted to transform his pagan realm,
centered on Kiev, into a European power. They attended
services in mosques and Latin-rite churches but were
ecstatic at the liturgy in Constantinople: "We did not know
whether we were on earth or in heaven. No earthly spectacle is more beautiful. And after having experienced such
sweetness, how can we return to the bitter? We will no
longer be pagans." This may be no more than a beautiful
story, but it expresses a truth: the choice of Byzantine-rite
Christianity by Vladimir was partly an aesthetic one.

The liturgy spoke just as plangently to novelist Marguerite
Yourcenar, who attended St. Nicholas Church in Leningrad
during a stopover there in 1961 and afterwards wrote:

From 10 A.M. to 1 P.M. we participated in a long and won-
derful service. In one corner, on a large table, women
changed and dressed children who had just received the
priest's benediction; nearby, in open coffins, the dead

119

awaited funeral rites. After the priest's prayer, one of the family drove the first nail in the coffin and a woman of fifty and two old ladies, who had married about 1910 in a world so different from that which they left, departed to forget their lives' events; and the children's cries persisted during the funeral liturgies. I have attended baptisms in St. Peter's. I have felt the beauty of sacraments received by one generation after another but here I felt close to the origins; I felt I was hearing the wheels of life and death turning as it must have seemed in the ancient mystery religions, in all the places where man felt near to the great, simple mysteries.

The Byzantine-rite liturgy makes a powerful appeal to all the senses and the imagination. For Eastern Christians, God is Beauty as much as Truth and Goodness. They still inhabit the Hellenistic world transmitted through Constantinople: the saints canonized in Moscow in 1988 were depicted in the elongated Byzantine style.

The Orthodox sense of the sacred nourishes a profound spirituality. It emphasizes surrender to God to achieve orthodoxy of the heart, an adherence to Christ free of legalism. By comparison, Latin Catholicism is disciplined and formidable, marching to the tune of a central authority. This struck home on a visit to Vilnius, Lithuania, in 1988 immediately after having been in Moscow. In Moscow's Orthodox churches the congregations had been devout and unorganized, but in Vilnius's Catholic churches they seemed serried ranks, punctual for the Mass which they diligently followed in their missals.

Orthodox sometimes complain that the Latin Mass is so swift and bare that they feel they have not participated in anything significant. For their part, Roman-rite Catholics often find the Orthodox Divine Liturgy overlong. The Roman rite tends to emphasize duty, as befits an institution which inherited the Roman Empire's legal tradition. This tradition has more rules than does Orthodoxy, where, for instance, there is no obligation to go to church each Sunday. Roman Catholic priests take vows of celibacy, but married men can become Orthodox priests (but not monks or bishops). Catholic spirituality is often linked to, and sometimes absorbed by, social activism, which has a weaker tradition in Orthodoxy. (Under Communism even comment on social issues was prohibited, increasing the identification of Orthodoxy with ritual.) Whereas the Orthodox are accustomed to an intuitive, synthetic approach to religious matters, the Western Church is at home with an analytic tradition which was reinforced at the time of the Reformation.

The French Orthodox theologian Olivier Clement has described the two traditions as follows: "The Church of Rome centralized to oppose the [Roman] empire but used the Empire's means. The Orthodox Church is more diverse, more conciliatory, but under the tutorship of the Empire or of all regimes which aspire to regulate it. And it becomes ever more static. What a mutual impoverishment!"

And he describes a further distinction, saying that Orthodoxy

> lacks the Western critical spirit, its ethical responsibility, its active charity in imitation of Jesus. The Latin Church lacks the Eastern's fully eucharistic ecclesiology, the unity of mystery and liberty in the Holy Spirit, the sense of divine energy, of the risen Christ who transfigures the whole man including his body and, through humanity, the whole universe. The tragedy of European Christianity is that the West has inspired an extraordinary historical dynamism but without the dimensions of a cosmic Christianity capable of illuminating the world explored by science.

Orthodox Churches are local or national Churches united by a shared faith, sacraments, and liturgy but without a central authority exercising jurisdictional power. The patriarchate of Constantinople is given a primacy of honor but does not have jurisdiction over other Orthodox Churches. Because they are typically identified with nationality, Orthodox Churches have little outside leverage against government pressure such as the Vatican can offer particular Catholic Churches.

In Russia, Peter the Great made the Orthodox Church virtually a government department. For their part, the Communists separated the Church from the state only to put it under state control. Until the end of the 1980s the K.G.B. controlled entry to seminaries and favored the advancement of those who were pliable.

Similar pressures were brought to bear in other Communist countries. Patriarch Teoctist of Romania, for instance, went into paroxysms of servility before dictator Nicolae Ceauşescu and resigned, but only briefly, after his fall. In Communist regimes there were some Catholic stooge bishops and some independent-minded Orthodox bishops, but on the whole Catholic hierarchies behaved more honorably.

The K.G.B.'s approach to seminarians was insidiously patriotic. Continuing a czarist-era practice, its functionaries asked simply to be informed about any seminarians with anti-state attitudes. Once a seminarian's promise to collaborate was signed, the K.G.B. had the informer in its hands. (Some Russian Orthodox clergy who studied at the Jesuit-run Pontifical Oriental Institute in Rome were in the awkward situation of having to report to the K.G.B. or face being recalled. Their solution was to send home information that had already appeared in the Italian press. The Jesuits took the fact that the students were reporting home as par for the course, saying they would be concerned only if there were students whom they had not identified as informing the K.G.B.)

Mykhaylo Havryliv is one who denounced K.G.B. influence within the Orthodox Church. Born in Ukraine in 1949, he studied at the Orthodox seminary in Leningrad under the historian and ecumenist Bishop Nikodim. Summoned to a K.G.B. office, Havryliv was asked to write a report on a fellow student. Uneasy about this, he consulted with Nikodim, who advised him to collaborate, saying that it did not harm the religious life and enabled attainment of greater things.

After a while, Havryliv kicked against the traces, refusing to collaborate further; a K.G.B. official told him he would never become a bishop. After he was assigned to a West Ukraine parish, K.G.B. agents in the Russian Orthodox Church asked Havryliv to write secret reports on other Christians, mainly Ukrainian-rite Catholics. In 1978 Havryliv himself became a Ukrainian-rite Catholic. Because he wrote a book about his choice, he was appointed to a cleanup crew in Chernobyl after the nuclear boildown. He was active as a Catholic priest and, during the millennium celebrations, was in the delegation that put the Ukrainian-rite case to the Vatican representatives at their Moscow hotel.

Havryliv claimed that Orthodox priests who worked hand-in-glove with the K.G.B. were allowed to travel, were entrusted with external and ecumenical relations, and obtained promotion readily. He also claimed that the Russian Orthodox External Relations Department, whose headquarters was at the Danilov Monastery in Moscow, was guided by K.G.B. officials. In Orthodox eyes, Havryliv is a deplorable turncoat, but similar criticisms have been made by Orthodox priests such as Gleb Jakunin and George Edelstein. According to them, the Russian Orthodox hierarchy was virtually the K.G.B. at prayer.

Incidentally, Bishop Nikodim lies in the St. Petersburg Holy Trinity cemetery near Dostoyevsky and could well have been a character in one of his novels. Some suspected that he was a secret Jesuit, some that he was a K.G.B. general, and some that he was both. He died of a heart attack in John Paul I's arms in the Vatican.

———

The split between the Eastern and Western Churches developed over a long period. Divisive theological and political issues as well as jurisdictional conflicts came to a head in 1054, and the gulf widened when Western crusaders sacked Constantinople in 1254. Reunification was attempted at the Second Council of Lyons (1274) and was achieved in Florence (1439), when it was agreed that Eastern Churches retain their liturgical traditions and canonical discipline while recognizing the pope. The Florence agreement, reached as Easterners sought Western military support against the Ottoman Turks, was not accepted when Orthodox delegates returned to their homelands, but it served as a model for later partial agreements.

At different times from the end of the sixteenth century, often because it was the only way to gain full civil rights under Catholic rulers, various segments of the Eastern Church united with Rome. They were called Uniate Churches, often with derogatory intent, but the word *Uniate* is adopted here because of its convenience. Conviction as well as duress had its part in this transfer of allegiance: there were Uniates who saw themselves as the true heirs of the original Eastern-rite Christians who had received their faith from Constantinople but recognized Rome because at that time they were united. They hoped to be forerunners of a movement which would eventually ensure all Eastern-rite Christians recognized the pope's authority, but they irritated the Orthodox, who considered them robbed by Rome in an act of ecclesiastical imperialism. And Rome was often diffident of the Uniates. "For the Orthodox we're traitors," said one exasperated senior Ukrainian-rite priest, "and for Rome we're hybrids."

Central and Eastern Europe is a tangled skein of races, rites, and faiths. Small Uniate communities exist in Bulgaria and the former Yugoslavia, but about six of the roughly seven million Eastern-rite Catholics are concentrated in contiguous areas of Central and Eastern Europe where frontiers have frequently changed.

After World War II, Communist governments suppressed Uniates in Romania, Czechoslovakia, Belarus, Poland, and

Ukraine. The Ukrainian-rite Church's experience is particularly significant, as it is the largest of all Eastern-rite Catholic Churches and was the world's largest outlawed religious group. (The Ukrainian Catholic Church is a sister Church of the Latin-rite and other Catholic Churches in full communion with the Holy See. The limits of its autonomy are disputed. It selects its bishops, who then have to be endorsed by the Holy See. But under Communism the process of appointing bishops took place in secret, and there was only intermittent contact with the Holy See. Its members sometimes grumble that the Holy See rides roughshod over them, discouraging any Orthodox considering fuller communion with Rome. They complain also that there is pressure against allowing their tradition of married priests to continue in the Americas, Western Europe, Australia, and elsewhere with immigrant Ukrainian communities.)

Ukrainian-rite Catholics are found mainly in what was formerly Galicia. It was part of the Austro-Hungarian Empire until World War I, then in 1919 passed under Polish control. It became part of the Soviet Union only with World War II. Its capital city, Lviv, has almost a million inhabitants. Nestling amid low hills, central Lviv has the air of a solid, pre–World War II town: broad streets, four-story buildings, and a fine opera house. But maintenance has been neglected for decades.

Initially, Soviet authorities recognized the Ukrainian-rite Church, whose faithful constituted about a seventh of Ukraine's population. But early in 1945 they cracked down on it, partly because they suspected that it supported the armed Ukrainian independence partisans. Archbishop Josyf Slipyj, who had become its metropolitan archbishop only the previous year, was arrested at night in Lviv, driven to Kiev, and sentenced to life imprisonment. It seems that he was being made to pay for the alleged Nazi sympathies of his predecessor, Andrey Sheptytsky. (Sheptytsky had studied in Munich and dealt directly with the German occupation forces to obtain favorable conditions for his people; he also protected Jews. The Soviets accused him of being pro-German but his attitude towards Jews contradicts this. His beatification process is underway.) Slipyj was suspected of aiding the Ukrainian independence partisans, but nothing was proved against him.

In March the following year, a "rigged" synod in St. George's Cathedral, Lviv, attended by no bishop and only 216 of the 3,000 clergy, decided to dissolve the Church and merge with the Orthodox. In all, 700 priests became Orthodox, 1,500 others were arrested, and the remainder went into hiding. For Soviet officials, the Ukrainian Catholic Church had ceased to exist, and the Orthodox Church agreed with them.

Although Pope Pius XII issued an encyclical in defense of the suppressed church, the world was reminded of it only in February 1963, when Soviet Premier Nikita Khrushchev allowed Josyf Slipyj to go to Rome after almost eighteen years in Soviet prisons and labor camps. Cardinal Johannes Willebrands, who went to Moscow to accompany Slipyj to Rome, has recounted their meeting in a corridor on the sixth-floor of the Modeva Hotel. "Are you Metropolitan Slipyj?" Willebrands asked the tall, powerfully-built, bearded ex-prisoner.

"I've been waiting for you for eighteen years," responded Slipyj. Willebrands found him "full of energy."

When Slipyj was born in 1892, his village was in the Austro-Hungarian Empire. He attended a seminary and taught in Lviv, where in 1918 the West Ukrainian People's Republic was proclaimed. It united with the Ukrainian National Republic of Kiev, but in 1919 Poland annexed Galicia and maintained control until World War II.

Slipyj said that he had been persecuted by the Bolsheviks, the Poles, and the Gestapo, but after a while he was tempted to add the Vatican to the list. He found imprisonment in the Soviet Union more bearable—in the Vatican he felt tied down by silken strings and struggled manfully to gain respect for his Church. It was paid the tribute of surveillance in Ukraine, but in Rome, he complained, it was unknown and ignored. To offset this, in Rome he built St. Sophia Church, established a Ukrainian "university" which was, in fact, a seminary, and insisted punctiliously on his rights and prerogatives, as they were those of his Church.

Certainly he was more attractive standing up to Soviet jailers than standing on his dignity over ecclesiastical protocol in Rome. Backed by many of the approximately one million Ukrainian-rite Catholics in the Americas, Western Europe, and Australia, he insisted on being considered a patriarch, but the Vatican demurred, mindful of Soviet opposition to Slipyj's plans, the foreseeable negative Orthodox reaction, and the likelihood that he would be taken as a nationalist leader. But in 1965 he was made a cardinal by Pope Paul VI. Slipyj died in September 1984, at the age of ninety-two. He was succeeded by Myroslav Lubachivsky, who had left Ukraine in 1939 and had become archbishop of the Ukrainian Catholics of Philadelphia.

In Ukraine itself, loyal priests who had not been imprisoned took jobs but in their spare time continued their ministry and even prepared seminarians. A core of faithful received sacraments only from these priests, but others went to Orthodox churches while still considering themselves Catholic.

One Soviet response to appeals for recognition of the Ukrainian-rite Church was to point out that Eastern Catholics could attend still-functioning Latin-rite Catholic churches. But Ukrainians identified these as Polish churches, and Poles had been the detested overlords before the Russians' arrival. Besides, many felt closer to the Orthodox, who had the same rite, than to Latin-rite Catholics, who were under the same papal jurisdiction.

In Eastern Christianity, rite has an importance which Western Christians find hard to comprehend. In a sense, the rite is Orthodoxy; it is both cult and culture. For the Orthodox,

Christian education is mainly through the liturgy. A crucial distinction is that Catholicism has one jurisdiction (Rome) but many rites, whereas Orthodoxy has one rite but many jurisdictions. The Latin rite is often considered synonymous with Catholicism but, in fact, there are sixteen rites among Churches in full communion with the Holy See, such as that of the Syro-Malabar Church in India. Even Milan has its Ambrosian rite. The largest of the non-Latin-rite Catholic Churches is the Ukrainian. The rub is that its liturgy is identical to that of the Orthodox Church.

Soviet authorities argued: "If you're faithful to Rome, worship in Latin-rite churches." Ukrainian Catholics responded: "We acknowledge the pope but must worship according to our Eastern tradition." They sensed that if they abandoned their tradition they would lose their identity. The implication of their response, however, was that one day all Orthodox might follow their example and recognize the pope.

A factor in the survival of the Ukrainian-rite Church was that Soviet officials in their reports downplayed its strength for fear of reproofs. Another factor was that Catholics with priestly vocations attended Orthodox seminaries without making their allegiance known.

West Ukraine was the USSR's richest region for priestly vocations, church buildings, and believers' offerings. Obviously control of West Ukraine was important to the Russian Orthodox Church. But at a time of increasing nationalism, many Ukrainians resisted the Russian Orthodox Church as a vehicle of Russianization epitomized by Metropolitan Filaret of Kiev who, although Ukrainian, preached in Russian. In contrast, the Ukrainian Catholic Church was seen as authentically Ukrainian. To offset this, in January 1990, the Russian Orthodox Church in Ukraine was renamed the Ukrainian Orthodox Church, although still ultimately dependent on Moscow. This did not convince many believers, but the autocephalous (self-governing) Ukrainian Orthodox Church, which had been destroyed in the 1930s, reemerged and won adherents. Sometimes Ukrainian Christians seem to be playing ecclesiastical musical chairs as they switch allegiance between one denomination and another. This can mean continuing to go to the same church building to attend the same liturgy with a change, as it were, only of labels.

Inspired by other Central and Eastern European human-rights movements, the Initiative Group for Defense of Believers' Rights was formed in Lviv in September 1982 to arrange petitions, meetings, and marches that would overcome believers' fear that they were isolated. It was strengthened in 1987, when Iwan Hel returned after fifteen years in Siberia for human rights activities. In 1952 Hel had been expelled from school for refusing to join the Communist Youth Movement. However he managed to graduate in history at Lviv university and then taught, before his spell in Siberia. Instead of cowing him, his years in Siberia seemed to have burned fear out of Hel.

In August 1987, 2 bishops, 23 priests, and 164 lay people signed an appeal to John Paul II and Mikhail Gorbachev, requesting legalization of the Ukrainian Catholic Church. They were the tip of an iceberg: behind them, it was claimed, were eight other bishops, a thousand clandestine priests, and some five million faithful. Everyone held their breath, but no action was taken against the signatories. It was de facto recognition. The Orthodox continued to deny the Church's existence, it had no recognized rights, but believers began to profess their faith in public, even if some were still persecuted. It seemed that Moscow had abandoned the Russian Orthodox, probably because Gorbachev wanted better relations with the Vatican.

On October 29, 1988, while celebrating the liturgy in the baroque Transfiguration Church of Lviv, Father Yaroslaw Chukhnij, thirty-six, announced that he was not an Orthodox priest, as it had seemed, but a Catholic. Subsequently the

parish representative bodies also declared themselves
Catholic—once again Ukrainian Catholics had a church in
Lviv. Pale-faced Chukhnij, who is married with four children,
said he had always been Catholic but had attended an Orthodox seminary as no Catholic one was available. After his
acceptance as a Catholic priest by Archbishop Sterniuk, his
family received death threats.

Hundreds of priests who had previously presented themselves as Orthodox were to declare themselves Catholic in the
following two years, while hundreds of nuns emerged from
living clandestinely. There were accusations of Ukrainian
Catholic violence against the Russian Orthodox. On a visit
from Moscow, Orthodox Father Gleb Jakunin, who earlier
had stood up for Ukrainian Catholics, warned that they
should not pass from being victims to making victims.

Ukrainian Catholics were gaining confidence but were dis-
concerted to find, now they no longer had to celebrate Mass in
private houses or in the woods, that the Vatican was negotiating with those they saw as their persecutors. At least that was
how many of them interpreted the decisions of the joint Russian Orthodox–Catholic Commission established as a result of
the first John Paul II–Gorbachev meeting; it met March 5–15,
1990, in Moscow, Kiev, Lviv, and again Moscow.

On 13 March, eighty-three year-old Archbishop Volodymyr
Sterniuk, who headed the Ukrainian-rite delegation, walked
out of the meeting saying he considered the negotiations
invalid. There had been a breakdown of trust. Ukrainian
Catholic participants felt they were not being treated as
equals as they had no recognized status. They were right.
They wanted not only recognition, but for the Orthodox to
admit to error in participating in the takeover of the Ukrainian
Catholic Church. They also wanted the return of all their
churches and property taken since 1946; before that date, the
Orthodox had only one church in West Ukraine, and they had
not built any afterwards.

The Vatican representatives were in a tricky situation. They were negotiating an issue which, until the previous year, Soviet authorities would have considered an internal matter and which was still considered such by the Orthodox. They did not want to seem merely the Ukrainian Catholics' big guns, as the issue of ecumenical relations with all Orthodox was at stake. Like the Russian Orthodox, but for different reasons, they wanted to confine the discussion to assignment of churches. The subtext was that the Ukrainian Catholic representatives should leave the fundamental question of their Church's recognition to dealings between the Vatican and the Soviet government. "Trust us" was the Vatican delegation's message. But the Vatican representatives also wanted time to look closely at these bishops they knew only by name. When in Lviv on March 12 all ten bishops met the Vatican delegation for the first time, the men from central office had asked each for a curriculum vitae.

The disappointment over the commission was all the more bitter because Ukrainian Catholics had suffered precisely because of their allegiance to the pope. Some faithful had doubts now about the pope, who after all was Polish and therefore the traditional enemy. In fact, John Paul II had championed the Ukrainian Catholics wholeheartedly, but some of them began to heed members of the autocephalous Ukrainian Orthodox Church when they asked: "What's the Vatican ever done for Ukraine?"

In Lviv, disappointment over the "betrayal" during the commission talks was replaced by joy at Easter 1990. An overflow congregation celebrated the Resurrection all night in the Transfiguration Church, then shortly after dawn went to a park on the city outskirts where a Carpathian mountain village is recreated in a hilly setting. Even after the advent of Communism, some had always gathered in the park to celebrate Easter Sunday. This, however, was a special feast: the sun shone; a throng attended; and for the first time in forty-four years, religious and folkloric celebrations alternated.

It was an affecting occasion: many of these people or their relatives had been exiled to Siberia, where some wrote liturgical books from memory to help keep their faith alive. Others had suffered for their faith in Lviv. They had been discriminated against at work, undergone house searches, made persistent but risky attempts to offset their children's atheistic education, and resorted to subterfuges to partake in the sacraments. Now they were celebrating their faith in the open, in a sunny public park. The stock greeting as friends met was a hearty "Christ is risen" and the response "He is truly risen."

The day began with an open-air liturgy sung by a splendid choir. An elaborate brunch was then served for Archbishop Sterniuk and sixty guests in a reclaimed Studite monastery. Smiling Our Lady of Mercy and St. Vincent de Paul nuns, in habits which until recently they had not been allowed to wear, served the many courses they had prepared as if they had been waiting almost half a century for the occasion. Sterniuk, who had presided over the night-long ceremonies in the Transfiguration Church, sat on a chair in the park as youths danced around him. Nearby other groups were dancing, playing games, or listening to a musical trio from East Ukraine who had come to express their solidarity with the West Ukraine democratic movement. There were men in Cossack costumes firing a toy cannon, and visits to a small zoo with a Carpathian bear. Buglers attracted attention for children who recited verse on a platform, then a vespers-like service was held. The folkloric flowed into the religious and religion melded with nationalism expressed by blue-and-yellow Ukrainian flags and flowers. Thousands participated, yet only a few months before, the Russian Orthodox Metropolitan Filaret had said that there was no such thing as a Ukrainian Catholic Church.

The former Lviv Museum of Atheism reflected the changed atmosphere. Its last moment of glory must have been when Sputnik did not find a bearded god in the heavens. After a

National Geographic article described it as a "chamber of horrors" (because of the tableaux of Inquisition tortures), the museum's garish displays had been toned down and it was shifted from a former Dominican church, which was preserved as an artistic monument, to its annex. It consisted of an account of the development of religions and atheism with examples of atheist propaganda such as photos of gross clergy repulsing starving peasants. One display showed a chalice, bags of wheat, and starving families with the equation underneath: one chalice = twenty-five bags of wheat = food for five families. It dated from the 1920s, when the Orthodox Church took up a collection and sold possessions to help famine victims but, as it refused to hand over liturgical vessels, was charged with indifference. (There was no reminder, however, of Stalin's chilling statement that "the bony hand of famine will stop the counter-Revolution.") The museum's curator, Volodymyr Hajuk, who described himself as a "historian and non-practicing atheist," said he intended to open a bookshop for religious and atheist books, which seemed rather like a shop selling both baby-walkers and condoms.

Changes had occurred also in the Lviv city administration. Prewar style survived in the mayor's office: polished parquet floors, graceful chandeliers, golden drapes, and a large, decorated ceramic stove. Early in 1990 the Democratic Bloc Town Council had thrown out the statues of Marx and Lenin. Catholic Basilian nuns made a blue-and-yellow Ukrainian flag which was blessed in the Transfiguration Church before being installed in the chamber. The mayor was sworn in on the Bible, and each Council meeting began with the Our Father.

Subsequently, many of the unresolved questions of the Ukrainian Catholic Church were settled. All Ukrainian bishops in their homeland were confirmed by the Vatican. Catholics regained St. George's Cathedral in Lviv and, in March 1991, after fifty-two years in Rome, Cardinal Myroslav Lubachivsky returned to Ukraine, transferring his headquarters there. Cardinal Slipyj's body was later brought from Rome to St. George's for burial. The Ukrainian Catholic Church obtained juridical recognition which entitled it to hire staff and to run orphanages, schools, and seminaries. It attracted seminarians at a higher rate than Catholic Churches in the West.

————

Josyf Slipyj once wrote that Eastern-rite Catholics have a unique experience of living "between two worlds, between two Churches, between two spiritualities." One result is that they combine elements found in Latin Catholicism and in the Orthodox Church: they have the strong Orthodox sense of the ineffable, but their link to Rome has given them a deeper social awareness, access to wider scholarship, and a reference point beyond the national context. As well as retaining the Orthodox monastic tradition, they have adopted Western apostolic activism. They also follow some Western devotional practices such as the rosary.

Living between two traditions and two cultures can be uncomfortable. And Eastern Catholics also live between two councils, Florence and Vatican II, which involves a gap of over five centuries. They are a result of the piecemeal policy (segments of the Orthodox Church recognizing Rome) which derived from the Florentine Council. They lived clandestinely with these convictions, but when they reemerged they found the Vatican Council had changed the Church's ecclesiology.

At the Vatican Council, Orthodoxy was recognized as a sister Church offering sufficient means of grace for salvation. Orthodox were no longer expected to return to Rome. Even when Catholic ecumenists considered that Communism in many countries had systematically corrupted the Orthodox through the secret police, they did not condemn the Orthodox Church as such. It had borne the brunt of Communist hostility when all Christians were considered fascists and class enemies. Many of its bishops were compromised, but its faith was uncorrupted. It has been said that Catholics could turn to the pope; Baptists, for a time, to Jimmy Carter; but the Orthodox had no one to help them fend off Communist pressure.

The Vatican Council proclaimed that Catholics and Orthodox share the same faith and sacraments. The problem was that, in ex-Communist Europe, they also shared the same churches or, rather, clashed over them. Catholics claimed back the churches which the Communist authorities had given to the Orthodox. But the Orthodox said that, after forty years, those attending them had become Orthodox and deserved churches. In Ukraine many were returned, but few were handed back in Romania where a census, which Catholics complained was rigged, showed that there were only 230,000 Catholics instead of the claimed million plus figure. There were nasty fights over property with each side accusing the other of violence.

The Uniates continued to suspect that the Vatican was prepared to abandon them to make a deal with the Orthodox or state authorities. The Romanian Cardinal Alexandru Todea clashed with his old friend Cardinal Johannes Willebrands, head what is now called the Pontifical Council for Promoting Christian Unity, over this issue at the 1991 synod in the Vatican. Todea warned vehemently, "Let no one say Uniatism is opposed to ecumenism." But many continued to say it. One Eastern-rite Catholic protested indignantly: "What I don't understand is that these Vatican ecumenists are embarrassed by our sufferings."

————

Perhaps the ecumenists were embarrassed rather by the Uniates' presence, for it certainly complicated their task. Those who created the Uniate Churches may have been too clever by half. Are they an historical sport and an ecumenical cul de sac, more hindrance than harbinger? They are vigorous, although some suspect the ethnic-nationalist element in this. Their grace under pressure is a strong title: the Vatican cannot abandon them even though its support is sometimes cautious.

Orthodox, however, see Vatican support for the Uniates as part of an aggressive policy designed to take advantage of the debilitated Orthodox situation. They consider it an aspect of the wealthy, well-organized West's invasion of their territory. They have always viewed Uniatism as an aggression which shifted the frontier between Catholicism and Orthodoxy eastwards. After Communism's collapse they found further evidence of aggressive intent in various Catholic pastoral initiatives and in the appointment of Latin-rite Catholic bishops and the arrival of Latin-rite priests in Russia. Perhaps some Orthodox bishops looked with nostalgia to the last years of Communism when Catholics were not coming at them from all sides. It seemed nothing had changed since authorities in Christian Constantinople preferred to deal, as the saying went, with the sultan's turban rather than with the cardinal's hat.

According to the Orthodox, the Catholic priests who were arriving were trying to convert Orthodox to Catholicism in what they called "parallel missionary activity." The Catholic response was that the priests' work was not with Orthodox but with Catholics and also with the many atheists seeking a faith and often finding it through the proliferating sects. Similarly, Catholics responded that bishops were appointed for Catholic communities (and perhaps, although this was not spelled out, to control over-zealous Catholic missionaries, who were sometimes lay people).

But the manner of the bishops' appointment gave offense. Although one of the more ecumenically-minded Russian Orthodox bishops, Kyril of Smolensk, had visited the Vatican only a month before the appointment, no one, from the pope downwards, had mentioned it to him. The announcement, therefore, was taken as evidence of Vatican duplicity. The Vatican had not informed state authorities either, on the grounds that there was no concordat which required this. It was a fait accompli. The embarrassed, unofficial explanation was that the Vatican was not used to the new recommended practice of prior advice to the Orthodox about pastoral initiatives. To make matters worse, initially Tadeusz Kondrusiewicz was sometimes referred to as Archbishop of Moscow; after protests, he was generally given his official title of Apostolic Administrator for the European Part of Russia.

The Orthodox made no secret of their anger. And the Vatican, which had at least pursued a coherent line towards Communist regimes in its *Ostpolitik,* now seemed of two minds, perhaps because there was no clear model for the Orthodox-Catholic relationship prefigured by the council. The pope had not renounced universal jurisdiction, and the Orthodox could not accept it, as had been the problem for about 1,500 years.

In response to Orthodox protests about Catholic activism, the Vatican Secretary of State, Cardinal Angelo Sodano, said the important thing was that Christ be preached, implying that the ecumenical chips could fall where they might. But at the same time there were ecumenists who said that Catholic aid for the East should go to Orthodox as much as to Catholics. Likewise some Catholic lay movements wanted to bring the Christian message to all in Russia, whereas the Jesuits founded a community in Moscow and set up a spiritual cultural center in Novosibirsk but carefully avoided any appearance of proselytism.

"I think we've learned from our errors," said the Australian Cardinal Edward Cassidy, who succeeded Cardinal Willebrands as head of the Council for Promoting Christian Unity. New guidelines for Catholic activities in ex-Communist Europe, which take Orthodox complaints into account, were prime evidence for Cassidy. And he was pleased also with the results of a Catholic-Orthodox joint theological commission which had met in Lebanon in June 1993. Initially the Uniates were far less pleased. They objected to its affirmation that Uniatism had now been abandoned as a method of achieving full communion between Catholics and Orthodox. Cassidy pointed out that the declaration also contained an important Orthodox recognition of the Uniate Churches' right to exist. In 1994 Cardinal Lubachivsky accepted it.

Although the Orthodox Churches are menaced by internal divisions (which can make them prone to using charges against the Uniates as a rallying point), as well as haunted by compromises during the Communist era, they are still influential. Moreover, Orthodox lay movements, forbidden under the Communists, are expanding. There are some student exchanges and ecumenical initiatives with other Christians that are beginning to break down mutually distorting stereotypes.

At the time of the millennium celebrations, the Russian Orthodox Church had 6,000 parishes, but by 1994 it had 15,810. This was less than a third of the 54,000 it had before the Russian Revolution, but still showed that institutionally the Church was recovering lost ground. Almost half of its 2,902 monasteries had been opened (or reopened) in the preceding two years. But while a quarter of the Russian population affirms belief in God, between 1990 and 1993 the number of those identifying themselves as Orthodox was halved. Unless convinced that its contacts with the Catholic and Protestant Churches and with the West as a whole are beneficial, Orthodoxy is likely to strengthen anti-Western tendencies. In several Eastern European countries, there are convergences between the Orthodox and post-Communists.

The Bosnian conflict exacerbated Catholic-Orthodox tensions because the Orthodox Serbs were convinced that John Paul was hostile to them. And they saw the Vatican ranged in defense of Bosnian Muslims, partly because of its fear that the conflict would encourage Islamic fundamentalism. The situation revealed both the urgency of ecumenism and its difficulties; for, in the Bosnian clash, the spiritual traditions which John Paul claims are complementary appeared instead to be a cause of conflict.

Other developments, however, benefited Catholic-Orthodox relations. Werenfried van Straaten, the Dutch Norbertine who had helped Germans after World War II and then extended aid to Catholics under Communist regimes through the Aid to the Church in Need organization, by 1993 considered reconciliation between Catholics and Orthodox as his greatest challenge.

In California, after a stay at the Catholic Eastern-rite Holy Transfiguration Monastery, he realized that

> the greatest obstacle to such reconciliation is the deep-rooted Russian mistrust of the West and the almost ineradicable conviction that the Vatican, partly by means of our aid, is trying to "buy" the Russian clergy in order to "latinize" Russia and deliver a mortal blow against the weakened Orthodox Church by a massive campaign of proselytism.
>
> This Orthodox phobia only becomes comprehensible in the dark light of the Fourth Crusade (1202–04) which ended with the Sack of Constantinople, and the sanctioning of this crime (based, it must be said, on false information) by Pope Innocent III . . . Instead of liberating the Holy Land from Saracen oppression, the Crusade became a barbaric war against Christian princes for the sake of political and economic power. With utter contempt for all that was not of the Latin Tradition, this shameful deed went hand in hand with the profanation of Byzantine churches, the doing to death or expulsion of the Byzantine clergy and their replacement by Latin clergy . . . To this day this crime is for all "Greeks" the irrefutable proof of the treachery of the Western Church and of her unyielding resolve to latinize all other churches.

Van Straaten called for a confession of guilt by the Western Church and reparation for the injustice as far as possible with a return of the plundered relics and treasures. (A first gesture had already been made under Paul VI when the head of St. Andrew was returned from Rome to the Ecumenical Patriarchate.)

Through Aid to the Church in Need, van Straaten also launched a program to provide a thousand dollar grant yearly for each of the 6,000 Orthodox and 60 Catholic priests in Russia. As there was a positive reaction from the Orthodox and a generous response from donors, financial support was extended to Orthodox as well as Catholic seminarians and to nuns of both denominations. In 1994, $3.5 million was donated for this purpose, but some benefactors did not approve of the initiative and later discontinued their donations.

Support is also being given for construction of a sanctuary (monastery, church, hostel, and old people's home) on the site of a former concentration camp at Achajir near Omsk in Asian Russia. Here, between 1937 and 1953, tens of thousands of prisoners were beaten, shot, tortured to death or died of starvation. Daily at 4 A.M. the dead and even the dying were taken by horse-drawn carts to mass graves, where the corpses were sometimes not covered with soil, so that the guards' pigs ate them. Many of those shot bore in their hands a seed from a local shrub; today thorny bushes grow where the victims lie. After Stalin's death in 1953, the camp was closed and attached to a state farm. Dimitry, the father of the farm's director Vitaly Meshcherniskov, had survived the camp. Vitaly did not work the camp land and, after Communism's collapse, ensured that it was donated to the Orthodox church.

In a keynote address in December 1994 to the Russian Orthodox council of bishops, Patriarch Alexy II praised some cases of financial aid from Catholics but also described them as isolated. He complained that Catholics had not kept their promise to inform Orthodox in advance of pastoral projects and accused the Catholic Church's top leadership of responsibility for aggression by Eastern-rite Catholics. He implied that the Catholic Church in Russia ("our canonical territory") should concern itself only with people of foreign origin such as Poles, Germans, and Lithuanians, using their languages.

But often Russian is the first language of these believers of foreign descent. The ancestors of many of the Germans, for instance, came to Russia before the first white settlers from England were transported to that warm Siberia, Australia. Many of those of non-Russian origin have lost contact with the language of their forebears. Russian Orthodox fear Catholic and Protestant use of Russian in the liturgy because the Orthodox are tied to Old Slavonic, which is barely comprehensible nowadays to many Russians.

A full Catholic-Orthodox accord still seemed not just difficult but impossible, but some Catholic and Orthodox were convinced that the impossible would simply take a little longer. They kept hoping against hope as did John Paul who, in May 1995, confessed his ardent desire for full unity in an encyclical *Ut unum sint* and in an apostolic letter *Orientale lumen:* "Every day, I feel a greater desire to go over the history of the Churches again, in order to write at last a history of our unity."

Chapter 10

On the Road

We came, we saw, God conquered.

John Paul II, quoting the
Polish warrior-king Jan Sobieski

During his first visit to a post-Communist country, Czechoslovakia, in 1990, John Paul II said that a united Europe was close at hand. His tone was less triumphalistic when he visited Poland and Hungary in 1991. Certainly there was still cause for rejoicing: except for the interwar years and, for Hungary, a period of virtual independence in the nineteenth century, both countries were independent for the first time in centuries, and the Church was free.

But, as John Paul noted, "freedom does not solve all problems." In Poland he emphasised that the past could be a springboard for the future; in Hungary he warned against being trapped by it. In Albania in 1993 he extended his hand to Muslims. In the Baltic States that same year he proposed the good ecumenical relations there as a model for other post-Communist countries. The initial post-Communist euphoria had evaporated, and he acknowledged in Riga, Latvia, that Communism had arisen in response to needs which had reemerged. In Croatia in 1994 he advocated ethnic reconciliation.

On his return to the Czech Republic and Poland in May 1995, he recommended that the Catholic Church admit its historical shortcomings, request forgiveness for the wrongs it had inflicted, and offer pardon for those it had suffered. As his reference point was the Reformation, it implied the necessity for Catholic-Protestant reconciliation to foster the European unity which had seemed imminent four years before. On other occasions he insisted likewise on Catholic-Orthodox reconciliation, but significantly none of his trips was to a country with an Orthodox majority. The visits showed how varied were the post-Communist situations and John Paul's response to them. Everywhere he was concerned that Christians, having won the war, might lose the peace.

———

What had foiled the high expectations in Poland? The Solidarity movement which John Paul had supported no longer spoke for the whole nation. It had attracted 10 million members as an expression of anti-Communist national sentiment, but with the demise of Communism it had split into its component parts. The industrial wing, which counted 2.5 million members, was determined to reduce political involvement in favor of trade union activities, where it had to compete with the OPZZ union approved by the past Communist regime.

The breakup of Solidarity was probably inevitable; more worrying was the disappearance of the Solidarity spirit. Under Solidarity auspices a dialogue had flourished between Catholics and non-Catholic leftists on matters such as the uses of power and the dangers of self-righteousness; this now had slowed. There was grumbling against the Solidarity-influenced government. Solidarity officials, lacking the glamor of the movement's founders, were described as "diligent ants."

The fact was that a heroic age had ended. And many were tired. "I'm only in my late thirties," said Adam Szostkewicz, an editor of the Cracow Catholic weekly *Tygodnik Powszechny*. "I've lived through the Solidarity saga: clandestine activities, fear of being discovered, imprisonment. It was exhausting. And I can understand younger people who do not want any of that—they just want to teach, be doctors, clerks, or whatever without having to sacrifice themselves for the nation. No people can live at that level of tension for long."

The Polish presidential campaign had revealed political immaturity in the vote for Stanisław Tymiński, who promised quick riches for all. He was beaten by Lech Wałęsa, who earlier had defeated Tadeusz Mazowiecki, a Catholic intellectual lacking the common touch.

Wałęsa's powers were hazy while constitutional revision was under way. This would touch the delicate issue of Church-state relations. Political groupings were fluid, and the first fully free elections were not held until October 1991. The government was attempting to switch from a command to a market economy without creating unemployment comparable to that in former East Germany. It achieved more against inflation than had the Communist regime. Lines no longer formed before most shops, but people complained that, whereas under the Communist regime they had money but no goods, now they had goods but no money. Free enterprise was evident everywhere, including the tailgate shops near Warsaw Station, one of which had as stock-in-trade three screwdrivers and a bottle of scotch. Commerce was preferred to production, where, it was claimed, Communist Party nominees still had a stranglehold. There were complaints that, while a few were becoming rich, the majority were now poorer. Economic indicators were a matter of fierce dispute, adding to the unnerving uncertainty. It seemed touch and go whether Poland would achieve a viable market economy, especially as the Soviet Union, which used to absorb a third of its exports, could no longer pay for them.

Some estimates of the number of abortions ran as high as 200,000 a year. A proposed law made anyone involved liable to imprisonment. Pornographic publications had made their appearance, and some championed pornography as a form of freedom.

"Maybe it was easier for the Church under Communism," said a Jesuit, Father Stanisław Musiał, in Cracow; "at least things were considerably clearer: the line between Good and Evil was sharp. Now it's more difficult for the Church which, moreover, runs the danger of seeming to block people's maturity."

In other words, under Communism the Church had an identifiable opponent, but now it had to handle the ambiguities of pluralism; what had been a redoubtable fortress had to become leaven. Under Communism the Church had gone from strength to strength, as indicated by abundant religious vocations: it was the only space of liberty for lectures and discussions; it witnessed to human dignity. Catholic publications, such as *Tygodnik Powszechny,* and the Catholic University of Lublin were oases of freedom.

But after Communism, who needed them? There were myriad free publications and university lecturers no longer had to parrot Marxist orthodoxy. Television now broadcasted real debates—Catholic publications or clubs such as those of Catholic intellectuals, which had been under the Church's umbrella, were no longer the only venues for free expression.

Moreover, rather than being a witness, the Church now seemed intent on giving lessons or imposing its views. Religious instruction, formerly a parish responsibility, was reintroduced in state schools, but other denominations complained they had not been consulted. Chaplains were again appointed to the armed forces. The Church gained access to the state broadcasting network and was held responsible for the punitive antiabortion draft law. The primate, Cardinal Józef Glemp, denied interference with the government or involvement in party politics, but complaints persisted that the Church was throwing its weight around. Some Catholics warned against ex-Communist turncoats becoming ostentatiously religious and the threat of an intolerant nationalistic Catholicism. Latin-rite Catholics in Przemyśl near the Ukrainian frontier were blocking the assignment of a church to Ukrainian-rite coreligionists. And anticlericalism was on the way back.

Although still over 50 percent, Church attendance was down by an estimated 20 percent, and the value of church offerings dropped compared to the mid 1980s. Under Communism the Church had seemed stronger than it was because it had temporarily attracted many who did not share its beliefs. But it had been excluded from various sectors of public life such as education and the media, which reduced its effective influence. Moreover, Communism's corrosive effects, for instance on the work ethic and the family, were widely felt. Now the Church's weak points were emerging.

The motto of John Paul II's visit in 1991 was "Rejoice and do not repress the Spirit," which meant "Thank God for Communism's downfall, but don't fall prey to new forms of materialism." In his nine-day tour of smaller and previously unvisited towns, John Paul showed pride in Poland's Catholic heritage as the cornerstone of the nation and tried to make history an inspiration for the present. In fact, the acceptance of the Catholic faith by the chieftain Mieszko at the end of the first millennium had led to his kingship and the nucleus of what was to become Poland. John Paul evoked the multiethnic, multireligious, multirite Polish commonwealth of the Jagełłon dynasty, which spread to the Black Sea, as a reign of tolerance and interior liberty contrasted to the religious conflicts in Western Europe at the time of the Reformation. He quoted King Sigismund II Augustus's words to his people, "I am not the keeper of your conscience," contrasting them with the contemporary Western European prince-people religious conformity.

The commonwealth had included Lithuanians, Belarusans, and Ukrainians. Thousands of them came to hear John Paul, whose itinerary took him near the Soviet frontier. He deplored the denial of liberties that his audience's forebears had once enjoyed, which may have raised hackles in the Kremlin. It seemed he was looking towards new territories to conquer or liberate. As Timothy Garton Ash wrote, when John Paul II talks of Europe he looks far beyond historic Central Europe, "way across the Pripet Marshes to the historic heartlands of Eastern Europe, to White Russia, even to the onion domes of Zagorsk."

His celebration of Polish history, as of his Slav origins, can cause misgivings. Some Slav regimes, such as that of Monsignor Jozef Tiso in wartime Slovakia, were harsh to other ethnic groups. And no matter how liberal commonwealths or colonialists are, there are usually indigenes who prefer that the master race go home. Casimir was a saint, but today there are intense anti-Polish feelings in Lithuania, Ukraine, and Belarus shared by some Catholics. It must be acknowledged that John Paul backed the Ukrainian-rite Catholics in Przemyśl, assigning them another cathedral when the Latin-rite Poles continued their occupation of the original one. These Poles saw the Ukrainians not as fellow believers but as heirs of those who had slaughtered Poles in World War II. "How much I want Catholics of both rites," said John Paul wistfully, "to love one another."

His pride in Poland's history and Catholicism made him angry at suggestions that Poland had to qualify for entry to Europe. "We do not need to enter Europe because we made it and we continue to make it with more dedication than others," he said and cited the assassinated Father Jerzy Popiełuszko as patron of Poland's presence in Europe.

In these statements, resentment at the fact that the West entered World War II to ensure Polish independence but concluded it with Poland assigned to the Soviet sphere may have erupted. A misunderstanding also seemed involved: obviously Poland is part of Europe, but what was in question was whether it would qualify for the European Union. John Paul II's words implied "we have proved our moral-spiritual superiority," but many Poles were more concerned with latching on to the European Union locomotive.

John Paul spoke daily about one of the ten commandments as if he were a new Moses who, in the words of Cardinal Glemp, had just crossed the Red Sea. On his trips he usually follows the local hierarchy's recommendations, but in his own country his talks probably reflected his personal assessment. He saw a need for a basic catechesis, including warnings against abortion, consumerism, and confusing liberty with licence. He deplored publicity and entertainment which "play with our human weaknesses" and also the "illusion of free love."

Passionately he denounced legalization of abortion, asserting that no parliament can legitimately endorse killing an unborn child. (Abortion was legalized in 1993, and an even more liberal abortion law was passed in October 1996). There was a consensus on the need to introduce a prolife law, but there was debate concerning its terms and whether it should be accompanied by other provisions for better housing and greater availability of effective contraceptives. But, on these issues, John Paul did not provide pointers.

He warned against consumerism destroying solidarity but, in impoverished Poland, this was rather like preaching against gluttony to the famished. There was sparce applause for the pope's words, as if many thought "let him who is without a swimming pool cast the first stone." John Paul also warned against economic development without respect for social justice, in which "everyone takes account of social interests as well as his own." This was fine as far as it went, but it did not go far. Frequently when economic problems are broached with Polish Catholic intellectuals they want to talk only about ethical aspects, which can seem an evasion. The urgent issue was to know how to apply principles, to decide how development could be achieved with the least social cost, but it seemed unreal to suggest that social costs could be avoided altogether.

Aware that the Church has to change in response to the changes in society, John Paul called for lay apostolic initiatives and an end to "the passive and consumerist style of using the Church's spiritual gifts." At the end of his trip John Paul said that "more than once Poles have shown that they can transform their love of liberty into creativity," but his fear that this time Poles might botch their opportunity loomed large. Perhaps he also realised that, while he had massive support when the Communist system was in place, now even many Catholics asked whether he had the answers to their new problems.

———

Warsaw's Cardinal Stefan Wyszyński was a loyal opposition to successive Communist governments in the sense that he would not push the contrasts to the point where they could provoke Soviet intervention. The governments recognized and even rewarded this attitude based on a consistent, although evolving, policy towards the regime.

In Hungary, by contrast, there was discontinuity. The phase of head-on regime-Church clash epitomised by the trial and imprisonment of Cardinal Mindszenty in 1948 was followed by a Holy See–government agreement, removal of Mindszenty, and appointment of László Lékai as primate. Lékai, who claimed to be applying the Vatican's *Ostpolitik,* obtained a series of small governmental concessions such as permission to send some seminarians for training in Rome. But he did not criticize the regime publicly. He seemed smug. A Hungarian priest, Imre Kozma, said the bishops usually clamped down on zealous priests as they wanted to keep on the right side of state authorities. Lékai's defenders say that Lékai's "little steps" policy was the only one possible when Catholicism, although having the allegiance of 60 percent of the population, was not nearly as strong as in Poland.

Unlike its Polish counterpart, the Hungarian Church was not prominent in the ferment which preceded the demise of Hungarian Communism. On the death of "little-by-little" Lékai in 1987, the primatial see went to the Franciscan László Paskai who proved almost as cautious as his predecessor. In an Austrian weekly, Paskai was quoted as saying that Mindszenty had mistakenly expected the Communist regime would not last and, because of this, the Church had lost its schools and the religious orders were suppressed. Paskai complained that he had been misreported, but the interview ranged him among those who considered the Church had been too intransigent initially, whereas the secretary of the Hungarian bishops' conference, Asztrik Vazsregi, considered the Church was later too complaisant.

The coalition government resulting from the first free Hungarian election was pro-Christian, but there was a large, mainly liberal, opposition to the Churches, indicated by the 30 percent parliamentary minority which voted against restitution of Church property seized by the Communists in 1948.

Some described approval for restitution of the property as a present to the pope. Another present for the pope was to find that, despite recent undynamic leadership, several lay Catholic reviews had been founded in the wake of Communism, the numbers requesting religious instruction in state schools had increased fifteenfold, and parents were demanding Catholic schools, which under new legislation were entitled to state financial support. The Communists had allowed the Benedictines, Franciscans, and Piarists each to run two boys' secondary schools while an order of nuns ran two girls' schools. The other, previously outlawed religious orders, helped by the government's decision to return monasteries and convents, were attracting recruits.

A significant trial concluded in May 1991. In the 1950s six members—four priests and two laity—of a Catholic group called *Regnum Marianum* were condemned to prison. They were involved in the youth apostolate, but this was considered conspiracy against the state. The Hungarian Supreme Court rehabilitated them, implicitly accepting their lawyer's argument that they were imprisoned for having taught youth "honesty, faith, tolerance, chastity, and loyalty" and that "today there would be less delinquency if these people had been allowed to carry out their work."

These words reflected a widespread conviction that the Churches were needed to combat moral laxness and delinquency, to reduce Hungary's high suicide, alcoholism, and abortion rates. In Poland there had been great expectations of the Church before the end of Communism; in Hungary, expectations had grown after its demise. But during the Communist era the number of priests was halved and their average age rose; it would take time to train new religious personnel.

No doubt aware of recriminations about the hierarchy's contrasting attitudes to Communism, John Paul recommended unity and advised the Church to concentrate on the future. Future orientation, indeed, was the most striking feature of his Hungarian trip. "We are leaders of communities called to move forward," he told the bishops, ". . . forgetting what lies behind." He warned against nostalgia and said religious practice in future would probably be less apparent than in the past.

"An immense expectation is sweeping the regions of Central and Eastern Europe," he told seminarians, "the people, disappointed by the ideologies which held sway until yesterday, are asking themselves what is the real meaning of life, asking themselves about truth, about God." He urged Hungarian Catholics to prepare themselves for this missionary opportunity by pursuing ecumenism, drawing up a national pastoral plan, holding diocesan synods, and encouraging small apostolic groups within parishes. As in Poland, he underlined the Church's public role and called for religious instruction in state schools.

In Poland and in Hungary John Paul reassured people that they could solve the problems of post-Communism, but he was anxious lest they fall under the sway of consumerist "practical atheism." But he was hopeful, and at a "meeting without frontiers" over which he presided at Częstochowa immediately before his Hungarian visit, he entrusted the situation's missionary opportunities to the youth who attended the rally.

And the youth responded. Svetlana Radioniva, for example, who was born in Omsk in 1963, had become curious about the Catholic Church in Siberia. She was not baptized, but she attended the Częstochowa youth rally because of the pope's claim that he offered the truth. Afterwards, she attended the theology course at the Jesuit faculty in Warsaw and was baptized. The Częstochowa rally was much more than just words in the wind.

———

When John Paul went to Albania in late April 1993 to ordain four bishops, he spoke of the Church's "resurrection" and also of its "liberation" from "suffocating" atheism and "unspeakable brutality" that had come when "defeat seemed imminent." From the time they gained power, Albanian Communists oppressed religion; in 1967 the Communist leader Enver Hoxha declared Albania the world's first officially atheistic state. (In 1993 his imprisoned widow reportedly said that this was partly due to pressure from Albania's Chinese allies.) Any expression of religious belief, public or private, was prohibited; and churches and mosques were converted into gymnasiums or stores. Because Catholicism was strongly structured and had international links and because its "capital," the northern city of Shkodër (50 percent Catholic), had been the center of anti-Communist resistance, it was particularly hard hit. Before Communism there had been two hundred priests and six bishops; by the time it was voted out in 1992, there were thirty aged priests, most of them infirm, and one sick bishop. Almost all the surviving clergy had spent many years in prison. The Church had been all but totally crushed; but unlike the Church in Czechoslovakia and Hungary, no Albanian clergy had collaborated with the regime. Another thing that distinguished the Albanian situation was that there had been no negotiations between the regime and the Vatican. Albanian Catholics had toughed it out completely on their own. In the southern seaport town of Valona, three Servite sisters had managed to remain together as a community in two small rooms of their former convent, keeping the Eucharist hidden. Near Shkodër two nuns, whose convent had been closed, lived together in a village maintaining what they could of their former practices, taking in sewing, and raising animals.

Saints survived although God was banned: on All Saints Day people gathered to pray in cemeteries. Anticipating the destruction of their churches, the faithful had buried their bells in fields. By 1991 the bells were disinterred and, even before churches were rebuilt, pealed again from makeshift supports. The hymn "Christus Vincit" was heard in the land still marked by 320,000 igloolike cement bunkers which Hoxha had built as defense against invaders, and still suffering the effects of decades of paranoid leadership.

It has been said that Albania has no economic problems because it has no economy. At the time of the pope's visit, unemployment in the towns was around 50 percent. Horses and carts were a common form of transport. But Albania had manifested some strengths. One was that the Democratic Alliance won a comfortable majority, enabling it to form a government without partners, whereas coalitions had been a cause of weakness elsewhere in ex-Communist Europe. Second, it managed to enact legislation that put some land into the hands of the peasants, who were still nearly 70 percent of the population. Together with substantial foreign aid, this avoided what had been the very real danger of mass starvation in Europe's poorest country (which was potentially rich, however, because of its mineral wealth and tourist possibilities). A third positive factor was the tradition of religious tolerance.

John Paul tried to build on this, linking religious liberty to the consolidation of democracy, which could develop, he claimed, only "in full recognition of some fundamental values based on the intangible dignity of persons and human life." Catholics had a key role in the development of the Albanian written language and literature, and the national hero was Gjergj Kastriota, called Scanderbeg, a fifteenth century Catholic prince who led the resistance to the Ottoman Turks. John Paul stressed Catholics' part in the Albanian identity, but he also built bridges to Muslims at a moment when Albania's tradition of religious tolerance—as everything else—was threatened by the nearby Bosnian conflict. Reports of Christians killing Muslims in Bosnia and threatening the ethnic Albanian majority in Serbia's Kosovo Province undermined Christian-Muslim relations in Albania and had already pushed the country into the Organization of Islamic States.

John Paul wanted better relations with the Muslims in an attempt to forestall fundamentalism. And he encouraged Albania's integration into Europe when events tended to push it further into the Islamic camp: the Church, he said, wanted to contribute to Albania's progress and its "insertion in the European context as is proper given its historical roots." In Albania his vision of a Europe conscious of its Christian roots was enlarged to find place for Muslims.

———

Marx was right: perhaps only John Paul II was prepared to suggest this in September 1993 at the University of Riga, where until the beginning of the 1990s all had been Marxists. John Paul said that the "kernel of truth in Marxism was the denunciation of the 'exploitation to which inhuman capitalism had subjected the proletariat since the beginning of industrialised society.'"

The needs Marx identified were real, but Marxism's responses were mistaken, John Paul continued, because they implied that "in the name of 'class' or of a presumed benefit to society, individuals could be oppressed or even eliminated." John Paul's comments were influenced by Polish Catholic intellectuals' prolonged attempt to appropriate Marxist insights. The discussion in his encyclical *Laborem exercens* of the relations between labor and capital seemed to owe something to Marx's early writings. This did not prevent many from being surprised by his Riga speech: not only those who had suffered atrociously under Communism, but also those who saw market forces as a way to foster democracy, criticised him. The Russian trade union weekly *Rubchaya Tribuna* called John Paul the world's "last true Communist."

Now that the battle against Marxism had been won, John Paul's target was the "inhuman capitalism" which had reemerged amid the ruins of Communism. He recalled the serious doubts he had expressed about capitalism in *Centesimus annus* if it is "a system in which freedom in the economic sector is not circumscribed within a strong juridical framework which places it at the service of human freedom in its totality." Societies, he added, need Catholic social doctrine, which is not a third way between Communism and capitalism but indicates "the unpassable limits and suggests possible ways so that the various political and economic policies . . . may be worthy of man and in conformity to the moral law."

In Latvia and Lithuania, living standards nose-dived immediately after the fall of Communism because these countries lost privileged relations with the huge Soviet market without establishing alternative one with the West. Governments of ex-Communists had been elected, presumably because of nostalgia for the more economically stable Communist era. John Paul recommended reconciliation, saying society could not be divided into winners and losers. However he added that ex-Communists could not just swim with the tide but needed to expiate errors. In Latvia and Lithuania, in fact, it was not easy to distinguish winners and losers: Communism lost but ex-Communists not only had political power but also great economic clout, partly because they privatized many state industries by selling them to themselves.

In both countries there were Christian Democrat parties (which in the elections before the papal visit polled 13.4 percent in Lithuania and 6 percent in Latvia), but the Catholic Church had not identified itself with them. Rather it had chosen the long haul of preparing laity in Catholic social doctrine. Some Catholics who had suffered under Communism disagreed with the Lithuanian bishops' decision not to oppose ex-Communists and not to support Christian Democrats but simply to recommend a vote for "honest and conscientious" candidates. Earlier, the bishops had been shrewd enough not to grab at the proposal made after his defeat by Vytautas Landsbergis, the architect of independence, that a Catholic prelate should be made president to symbolize national unity. The new archbishop of Vilnius, Audrys Bačkis, who had worked in the Vatican Secretariat of State for many years, had a key role in avoiding any attempt at a repetition of the prewar direct Church influence on politics. John Paul deplored both exclusion of the Church from public life and clericalism.

The bishops were steering clear of clericalism, but the country was in limbo, waiting for a post-Communist political class to emerge. The immediate effect of savage capitalism was that those on fixed incomes got poorer as inflation rose while the few rich became richer and flaunted it. Once again, as elsewhere in post-Communist Europe, John Paul warned against the consumerist mentality; but once more it was somewhat like warning the Irish during the famine that they should not gorge on potatoes. With consumerism he linked moral permisiveness, life styles which indulge selfishness, and religious indifference.

John Paul tried to build on the prestige the Church acquired through its nonviolent resistance to Communism (the large number of seminarians was a pointer to this prestige). A positive aspect of post-Communist Baltic Christianity is the excellence of ecumenical relations there, a model for Christians elsewhere in post-Communist countries. This atmosphere may have facilitated relations between John Paul and a representative of the Moscow patriarchate who accompanied him. John Paul agreed with the Orthodox representative that history books containing misunderstandings and distortions of the relations between the two Churches should be revised. The already good ecumenical relations had been strengthened in Lithuania when the Orthodox bishop of Vilnius promptly backed independence. The Orthodox are a smallish minority (9 percent) whereas Catholics are almost 80 percent. In Latvia the Lutheran majority (50 percent), Catholics (25 percent), Baptists, Orthodox, and Old Believers (an Orthodox denomination whose members are predominantly ethnic Russians) collaborate in many fields, from producing a weekly paper in Russian as well as Latvian and also television programs, to preparing together a core course for religious or ethical instruction which is obligatory in Latvian schools.

Collaboration bridges the Latvian–resident Russian gap, which is a major problem in Latvia (35 percent ethnic Russians; a parallel problem exists in Estonia with its 30 percent ethnic Russians but not in Lithuania with only 9 percent Russians). Latvians and Estonians feel the more prolific Russians are a threat to their national and cultural identity; for their part, Russian residents feel they are second-class citizens without guarantees for their social and economic rights. Russians saw themselves as liberators of the Baltic States from the Germans who occupied them for three years in World War II, whereas the Balts saw them as colonialists. One Baltic family in five has had relatives deported to Siberia. Tens of thousands of Red Army officers retired to Riga, where they enjoyed a privileged status. Hundreds of thousands of workers were brought in from the Soviet Union as factory fodder; locals refer to them as "grey sludge." The issue was complicated by the presence of Russian troops (7,000 in Latvia and 20,000 in Lithuania) who outnumbered local forces. In accordance with prior agreements, those in Lithuania were withdrawn just before John Paul arrival, but Boris Yeltsin said troops had to be maintained in Latvia and Estonia because there was no accommodation for them at home and they were needed to protect the Baltic Russians.

In his first visit to territories which had been part of the Soviet Union, John Paul argued for the Russian residents' rights; and, when addressing intellectuals in the Estonian capital, Tallin, he criticised language being used as a barrier rather than as "an instrument of identity" (language tests were proposed for ethnic Russians requesting citizenship). His challenge to extreme nationalists was one of the high points of a trip which marked a shift in his interpretation of the changes in Central and Eastern Europe.

"The kernel of truth in Marx," the most striking part of this shift, indicated a move from simply celebrating the collapse of Communism to acknowledging that it arose out of real needs. Another shift in emphasis was that whereas in *Centesimus annus* John Paul had said the "true cause" of the fall of Communism was the "spiritual void brought about by atheism" at Vilnius University he described militant atheism not as the basic reason but "as one of the more important reasons" that Marxism produced an "iron dictatorship." He listed as other errors a "materialistic concept of history, a harshly confrontational view of society, the 'messianic' role attributed to a single party, the master of the state." Although the two passages are not strictly comparable, the differences between them reflected a more complex and nuanced interpretation.

One should judge no less seriously, he added, "what took place on the opposite side, the 'rightwing' regimes, that in the name of the 'nation' and 'tradition' likewise scorned the dignity which is proper to every human being regardless of race, conviction, and personal qualities." He mentioned Nazism, but his description could apply also to some past fascist regimes in "Catholic" countries.

All told, in the Baltic States John Paul II presented a version of the rise and fall of Communism which recognized that it was a response to problems still unresolved in "unsound democracies" and that its demise had triggered new threats such as policies of exclusive ethnicity.

———

In the former Yugoslavia, torn by the application of exclusive ethnicity policies, John Paul hoped to make a visit of reconciliation in September 1994. But it was truncated: because of security risks, he was not able to go to Sarajevo, which would have culminated his melding of current affairs and religious affairs, but even his attempt to go drew attention to its suffering. Serbian hostility prevented him visiting Belgrade.

His trip was thus confined to Croatia, where he celebrated the ninth centenary of the establishment of the Zagreb archdiocese; this tended to reinforce the Serbian opinion that he supported Catholic Croatia against Orthodox Serbia. He reaffirmed Croatia's right to independence, but just as firmly recommended that Croatian Catholics (who constituted about 75 percent of the population, which turned out in force; in Zagreb an estimated 750,000 attended the papal Mass, many of them wearing "John Paul defend Croatia" T-shirts) become apostles of "a new concord" between Balkan peoples.

Perhaps President Franjo Tudjman had expected more encouragement for Croation nationalism, but instead John Paul invited Balkan peoples to have "the audacity to forgive." Emphasising the ties of language and Slavic origin between Croatian Catholics, Serbian Orthodox, and Muslims, he said that religious belief "must return to be a unifying and beneficial force," a note he struck again during his visit to Slovenia in May 1996.

———

In September 1996 on his second trip to Hungary, John Paul maintained that the Church's spiritual message has beneficial civic consequences. He advised Christians, in the "confused" and "arduous" post-Communist era, to draw inspiration from martyrs and witnesses such as Bishop Vilmos Apor of Győr, who "offered his life for those entrusted to him"; Cardinal József Mindszenty; a doctor to the poor, László Battyányi Strattman, a "true hero" of charity; the priests and religious who suffered "long years of imprisonment and humiliation" under Communism; and also laity who were courageous at that time.

Vilmos Apor (1892–1945) was a baron who gave his own lands to the poor and showed constant concern for the welfare of workers. During World War II he wrote a pastoral letter in defense of the Jews. He died from three wounds inflicted by pistol shots while defending, on Good Friday 1945, young women who had sought refuge from drunken Soviet soldiers in the cellar of his residence. His beatification is imminent.

In ecclesial affairs, John Paul noted positive aspects: more fervor in religious orders, an increase in vocations, reorganization of the charitable organization Caritas, foundation of associations of Christian intellectuals, more Catholic centers of education and student residences, greater Catholic presence in teacher-training colleges, and growth of a

Catholic university revived after the demise of Communism. But he noted negative aspects too, such as the slow return of individuals to religious practice and the slow return of schools and other Church institutions confiscated during the Communist era.

Warning against allowing "pessimism, resignation, and unease" to take the upper hand, he had to heed his own advice. He was visiting the diocese of Győr and the Benedictine Abbey of Pannonhalma, which was celebrating its thousandth anniversary. It was founded before the split between Orthodoxy and Catholicism, and he had tried to arrange there his first meeting with the Russian Orthodox Patriarch Alexy, but Alexy did not come, reportedly because of opposition within the Synod of the Russian Orthodox Church. Communism had crumbled, but John Paul had still not achieved his second aim of winning the confidence of the Orthodox.

He had traveled a long road from the exultation of his trip to Czechoslovakia in 1989 when, because of the defeat of official irreligion, it had seemed that all problems were on the way to solution.

Chapter 11

It's Easier to Suffer

Many Christians in post-Communist Europe have found that, in the words of the Russian poet Irina Ratuskinskaya, "It's easier to suffer than to catechize." Persecution imposes stark choices. Rebuilding afterwards is a lengthy, complex process in which many issues appear fudged. And the intransigence needed to resist persecution is often unsuitable for the ambiguities of pluralist democracies.

Christians had to adapt to abruptly changed situations. East Germany, where an estimated 75 percent of the people were not baptized, became one with West Germany, where the overwhelming majority were Protestant or Catholic. The appointment of bishops in Siberia and elsewhere in the former Soviet Union meant an end to priests there roving virtually freelance; another change was the exodus of ethnic German Catholics, accepted in Germany itself, from the Asian part of the former Soviet Union. Freedom has meant fewer Catholics there because Ukrainians, Lithuanians, and Poles also have left for fear of violence or simply to return to their homelands. What was the hinterland of an atheistic regime has become the frontier of fundamentalist Islam.

In European Russia, some of those prominent in the Christian Seminar moved into politics. Aleksandr Ogorodnikov of Moscow became president of the Christian Democratic Union, which split after a poor electoral showing. Subsequently Ogorodnikov opened a soup kitchen, where he told the needy that the food was donated by Westerners who consider Russians their brothers in Christ.

Another seminar member, Vladimir Poresch, said scathingly that dull sermons might be more effective than the former atheist propaganda in killing people's hopes in the Church. In mid 1993 he became director of an Orthodox-sponsored Human Rights Institute in St. Petersburg.

During the August 1991 putsch attempt, Gleb Jakunin appeared on television screens worldwide atop a pro-Yeltsin tank. Jakunin, who claims to have been forced into politics by the hierarchy's hostility, is a Russian parliamentary deputy and an adviser to Yeltsin on religious matters. In 1992 he dropped a bombshell by announcing that K.G.B. files showed some Orthodox bishops had acted as K.G.B. agents; this brought the criticism that he had become vengeful. In 1993 he was unfrocked because he had participated in the parliamentary elections. Accepted as a priest by the breakaway Kiev Patriarchate, he applied for reinstatement with the Moscow Patriarchate but was advised that if he did not repent he would be excommunicated.

Nijolė Sadūnaitė, who had been exiled to Siberia for her work on the Lithuanian *Chronicle of the Catholic Church,* was disinclined to believe ex-Communists had a change of heart. After Algirdas Brazauskas, the former Communist Party secretary, won the first round of the 1992 elections, she told a crowd outside Parliament that "God and the Virgin Mary have turned their faces from Lithuania" and predicted that Communist rule would be accompanied by a spate of abortions. In Vilnius in 1993 she made news by publicly tearing up pornographic publications. She continued to irritate authorities, now not Communists but bishops. "She wants to tell bishops and priests how they should vote," said one bishop, adding, "you journalists have made a legend of her."

Another Lithuanian likewise suspicious of ex-Communists was Father Alfonsas Svarinskas, who as a seminarian had been exiled to Siberia, where he had assisted a fellow internee, Archbishop Josyf Slipyj. On return home Svarinskas inspired many to stand up to Communist oppression and cofounded the Committee for the Defense of Believers' Rights. After release in 1986 from the last of three prison terms totaling twenty-one years, he held a press conference in Rome. His thin face and twisted mouth gave him a dyspeptic look. He delivered one memorable throwaway line: "We don't insist on the immediate return of our commonwealth" (the Polish-Lithuanian Commonwealth which, in the fifteenth century, spread from the Baltic to the Black Sea).

At Svarinskas's trial in 1960, one of the prosecutors was the Communist Egidijus Bickauskas. In 1990, Bickauskas became the Lithuanian ambassador in Moscow, where he helped improve relations between the two countries. In 1992 opinion polls he was Lithuania's most popular public figure. Understandably, Svarinskas was indignant at his former prosecutor's continued presence in public life. He himself had a spell as a parliamentarian. He was a radical nationalist, described by Anatol Lieven in *The Baltic Revolution* as "a Torquemada-in-waiting, a vehement clerical nationalist extremist who had called, among other things, for the mass execution of former Communists on the pattern of the execution of Nazi collaborators in France in 1944." After leaving parliament he was made a military chaplain; it may have been only a coincidence, but shortly afterwards the Red Army withdrew from Lithuania.

Kazimierz Swiatek, who had worked in Soviet gulags in the Arctic circle, after his release in 1954 served as a priest in his native Pinsk for forty years. At the age of seventy-six, he was made archbishop of Minsk-Mohilev, succeeding Tadeusz Kondrusiewicz, who was transferred to Moscow. Like Kondrusiewicz, Swiatek was not allowed by Belarusan authorities to move to Minsk, the capital. He continued to live in a wooden house in Pinsk, pursuing his hobbies of making

8 mm. films and looking after two stray dogs he had taken in, while maintaining a strenuous pastoral schedule.

At eighty, in November 1994, he was made a cardinal and in 1995 the Belarusan authorities allowed him to transfer to the capital, where he lived in two rooms in the curia, a little cramped perhaps but certainly better than his previous accommodation in Minsk as a prisoner under the K.G.B. offices. Pinsk is in the borderlands where people had been deported but also frontiers had been moved. It had been in Poland when Swiatek was a child but after the war was part of Belarus, an area where the Polish and Catholic proportion of the population had increased to about 25 percent because of the border alterations. The Belarusan authorities have been uneasy about the increased Catholic-Polish influence, but permission for Swiatek to transfer to Minsk indicated a more positive attitude, so too did public recognition of Catholic as well as the customary Orthodox feast days. Permission was also given to reopen the seminary in Pinsk.

Swiatek paid tribute to the common people who preserved Christianity in the former Soviet Union—"those babushkas who gathered secretly, in cemeteries for the most part, to hum hymns"; but he found that Communism had destroyed social consciousness and left a spiritual void. He claimed that democracy is no panacea because it puts power in the hands of grey, amorphous *homo sovieticus,* the product of a society which tried to obliterate the past and cut all roots. As a result, "Soviet man" lacks the wisdom of earlier generations and has no sense of personal responsibility, pride in work, or creative flair.

"Unfortunately even many believers deserve this label," added Swiatek who, despite a heart attack a few years earlier, was still vigorous. The cardinalate is a long way from the Arctic Circle gulag, but he still keeps the ceramic cup which was his chalice there.

Archbishop Volodymyr Sterniuk, who had led the Ukrainian Catholic Church on the spot during the Communist era, found it hard to step aside on the return from Rome of Cardinal Myroslav Lubachivsky. At times Sterniuk appropriated the title of Metropolitan Archbishop, which is Lubachivsky's, and even had it incorporated in a seal he used. In 1991 he announced that he had appointed a bishop for Russian Catholics. The person concerned, Vikenty (his full name is Viktor Vladimirovic Cekalin), was known in Western Europe and in the Vatican, which did not give him credence, but he convinced Sterniuk that he was an Orthodox bishop who wanted to become a Catholic. When Communist rule prevented communication with Rome, bishops had been able to consecrate others pending eventual approval by the Vatican (and, in the case of Ukrainian Catholics, also by their Metropolitan, who was living in Rome). But these conditions no longer existed.

Sterniuk, who had lived all his years as a bishop under these conditions and then was disappointed by the Vatican's treatment of Ukrainian Catholics, acted as if he had full autonomy. Cardinal Lubachivsky issued a statement that Vikenty could not be considered a Catholic bishop, but for a time he acted as such. The obstinacy which had been Sterniuk's strength under Communism betrayed him in the changed circumstances. (By 1995 Vikenty was a priest of the Traditional Anglican Church in Queensland, Australia.)

Father Simon Jubani continued to fight a good fight without realizing it was time to stop. Resistance to Communism had trapped him into intransigence, making him seem in the new situation more a political brawler than a witness to the faith. Interviewed in his brother-in-law's home in Shkodër, silver-haired Jubani, who has a slight stutter, a strong angular face, and an athlete's limberness, said that the only effect of his years in Albania's harshest prison was loss of teeth from "eating a Communist every day."

He still found Communists everywhere and publicly denounced them. For instance he denounced Peter Arbnori, the Speaker of Parliament and one of its few Catholics, who spent twenty-six years in prison with him, as a thief and puppet in the hands of Southerners. In Jubani's opinion Southern Albanians systematically discriminated against Northerners. The charges against Arbnori arose out of the nightmare world of political prisons. Jubani also denounced the Muslim President of the Republic, Sali Barish, as a puppet of the Southern clan. Under the Communist regime Jubani stood up to a dictator, whereas now he was a free priest tearing into elected representatives. Formerly he embarrassed president Enver Hoxha; now he was embarrassing Catholic bishops, which may explain why he was not made one.

Unlike Jubani, Václav Malý left politics behind after Communism melted into air. The son of a Czech high school teacher, as a teenager he was convinced by the Warsaw Pact's invasion of Czechoslovakia that Jesus, rather than politics, was humanity's only hope. "Jesus is not an escape from difficulties," he said when interviewed at his Prague church, "but our only real source of strength."

Because of his involvement in the group Charter 77 and the Committee for the Defense of the Unjustly Persecuted, Malý was imprisoned and denied a government license to work as a priest. On release he became a stoker for Prague's coal-fueled hotels. "During the 1980s," he recalled, his impish nose wrinkling, "I kept tourists warm."

At the huge meeting in Prague's central Wenceslas Square which celebrated the end of Communism, he was the moderator. Like other Charter 77 members he could have obtained an important public or political position but instead returned to the priestly ministry which had been denied him for eleven years. "Now the Church must rely on its internal strength rather than being united with all opponents of the regime," he said. "It offers essential moral values: belief in sacrifice for others, in trust, in pledges, in faithfulness, all things which Communism corroded. The Church teaches people shared responsibility, which is crucial if democracy is to work." In December 1996 he became auxiliary bishop of Prague.

Under Communism, Tomáš Halík had prepared for the post-Communist era but had not foreseen that for some coreligionists it would be an occasion to reaffirm the past. Born in 1948, Halík was the only child of a Prague publisher's editor responsible for the standard edition of Karel Čapek's novels and plays. He did not receive any religious education but at sixteen became interested in St. Augustine's writings. Then G. K. Chesterton's *Orthodoxy* made an impact, and he followed it with a diet of the works of Georges Bernanos, Graham Greene, and François Mauriac. He attended organ recitals in a church because he was intrigued by "a metaphysical culture which contrasted sharply with grey, Communist life." He also met a cultured, humorous priest not harried by the police, perhaps because his brother had been an idealistic Communist killed in a German concentration camp. This priest received Halík into the Church on his first day as a student of the philosophy faculty at the Charles University, Prague, where he became close to Ján Patočka, the philosopher who inspired the Charter 77 movement.

As Alexander Dubček's comparatively liberal government was in power, Halík was allowed to write a thesis on the Church's social teaching; he also qualified as a psychologist and psychotherapist. At the graduation ceremony in the university's Great Hall, Halík was asked at the last minute to take the place of an absent Communist speaker. He commented on a quote from Čapek that "truth is more powerful than power" and was warmly applauded. He was appointed a psychologist in a chemical industry planning department but, after a month, was asked to account for his "provocative" graduation speech. As the management backed him in his argument that those who found his speech provocative implicitly identified the regime with falsehood, he was not punished.

While lecturing in the psychology of management, he began to study clandestinely for the priesthood, for he felt that under Communism Czechs were spiritually starved. During a trip to East Germany in 1978 he was ordained—such away-from-home ordinations were one of the ways the clandestine Church evaded Communist constraints. While working as a psychotherapist with drug and alcohol victims he functioned as a priest.

He persuaded Cardinal Tomašek to launch a ten-year renewal program to culminate in 1997, the millennium of the death of St. Adalbert, the first Czech bishop of Prague, who also brought Catholicism to much of Poland. "We were the only group with a vision of the future and a plan for it when Communism fell," Halík said.

Halík pointed out that while the Church tended to become a ghetto under hostile regimes, the Czech experience forced Catholics to open out to others. For one thing, priests in prisons and factories made contacts which previously would have been unthinkable; for another, underground publications brought them into dialogue with all those who opposed the antihuman regime. The "limit experience of totalitarianism," he added, had convinced many nonbelievers that secular humanism was just not enough. Even if they did not convert, they acquired respect for Catholicism.

People like Halík had to start from scratch in finding out what a priest was meant to be, with the result that they were free of clericalism: "My relationship with the laity was based on total trust—my liberty and perhaps my life were entrusted to them because only they knew I was a priest. (Although I was living with my mother, I didn't tell her I'd become a priest as I didn't want to create difficulties for her.) We had to rethink everything in dialogue with people such as Václav Havel. The lesson I drew was that faith gives the strength to face reality."

Trust between priests and laity as well as dialogue with nonbelievers were good foundations for the post-Communism

Church, but it ran into new problems. "Decent people who refrained from criticizing the Church during Communism, in case the authorities took advantage of their comments, do so now, which surprises and offends certain Catholics. Some nuns who were resourceful and flexible under Communist pressure have changed, now that they can wear their habits again and have returned to their convents. They improvised for decades, now they want to teach younger nuns how it was in 1945. They say that's what's normal but such normalization creates problems for some recruits."

"Normalization," the word used to describe Gustáv Husák's reversal of all the innovations of Dubček, probably strikes a wrong note for Halík. "What's 'normal' for the Church is a big question," he continued. "I was twelve years a priest before donning clerical dress or saying Mass in vestments at an altar."

Halík, who was secretary of the Czechoslovakian Catholic Bishops' Conference for two years from 1990, continued: "I regret the time we devoted to discussing financial problems such as the best way to sustain the clergy or about property being returned to the Church—property which in some cases is merely a burden. Admittedly they were important issues, but in clandestinity we didn't have to worry about them. Of course, we have to adapt to new circumstances but also hold on to the positive things we learned under Communist pressure."

When Sonya Hlutkovsky, born in Pittsburgh of Ukrainian origin, took up residence in Lviv as press officer for Cardinal Lubachivsky, she found that the Ukrainian-rite Church of over four million members had only one administrative building, with a staff of forty, and one phone. After the Church's suppression, other chancery buildings had been used to accommodate families and the former seminary had become a post office.

"For forty years up to the collapse of Communism," said Sonya, "priests had been running into houses after work to celebrate Mass, quickly anoint the dying, or baptize infants. It was admirable that they did this after a day as garbagemen, stokers, ratcatchers, or what have you. But it didn't prepare them for helping people to face their day-to-day problems such as living with an alcoholic relative.

"Our priests are learning that there's more to their task than suffering, praying, and administering sacraments. And our bishops are learning that there's more to their mission than ordaining priests. When the Church was clandestine, there was no opportunity for priests to prepare people for marriage, but now it's both possible and necessary. Along the same lines we have to combat abortion. Here the basics of the faith have to be explained to people and related to their day-to-day life."

Sonya spotted attitude problems: "For too long people have been isolated and on the defensive, which makes it hard for them to understand the Vatican Council. They also lack any perspective on their situation, thinking all Westerners roll in wealth. The Church has to help offset the effect of decades in which everyone suspected everyone else of spying on them. It's made people unfree; they can't be open or creative."

Teachers at pontifical universities in Rome have made similar comments about seminarians from Central and Eastern Europe. "The striking thing," said a professor at the Jesuit Gregorian University, "is that academically the students are adequate but they're loath to take responsibility or initiative. They're disinclined to believe what they read or to act on it. If you put out a notice, they'll ask what's behind it."

The subterranean suspicions surfaced when a religious order brought its priests from Central and Eastern Europe to Rome shortly after Communism collapsed. "Some people weren't willing to communicate fully even with their confreres," said a Western participant. "They had learnt to be extremely cautious: years ago Communists infiltrated their formation program with devastating results. This caution makes them tend merely to parrot Church teaching instead of adapting it to new circumstances. They suspected that we

were either ingenuous or fellow travelers if we spoke of initiatives for peace and justice because these were favorite
Communist propaganda themes."

Priests prepared clandestinely often have little idea of what
jurisdiction means or how Church structures function. A
Ukrainian Catholic auxiliary bishop told his ordinary that he
had reached an agreement with civil authorities to establish
his own diocese. It had to be explained to him that new dioceses were not created in this way. Some underground-trained
priests have to be told they cannot just begin building a
church or set up a parish without consulting anyone. They
find it hard to realize that the days of "first thing that comes
to mind" pastoral activities are over.

———

By 1994 Catholics of the West were contributing annually an
estimated $60 million or more for pastoral and social-charitable
projects in post-Communist Europe. Countless organizations
were involved but the doyen was the international relief agency
Aid to the Church in Need, headquartered in Germany. In 1994
it sent a little over $25 million in aid to Central and Eastern
Europe and in 1995 the figure was $28.5 million. Since the col-
lapse of Communism, it had doubled its aid to Central and Eastern Europe without diminishing that to the Third World.

The German-speaking bishops (in Germany, Austria, and
Switzerland) weighed in with a similar yearly amount to Aid
to the Church in Need. In 1993 the German laity, partly
because reunification had made them aware of the difficulties
of reconstruction after Communism, established a project to
promote European unification by social-pastoral projects in
Central and Eastern Europe. Called Renovabis (Latin for
"you shall renew"), it has the bishops' support and is funded
by an annual Sunday collection but benefits also from government funds and funds previously channeled through a

Vienna-based aid organization. By the end of 1994 it had given financial support to 1,200 projects including publishing, student exchanges, and equipping Catholic seminaries and schools. In the first ten months of 1994, $13 million had been donated, which was a substantial increase on the previous year, and the German Bishops' Conference added half as much again.

In 1991 the U.S. Catholic Bishops' Conference initiated an annual Sunday collection which in three years brought in over $20 million, funneled through the Office to Aid the Catholic Church in Central and Eastern Europe, whose director Father R. George Šarauskas said, "all that we take for granted in the life of the Church—whether it's Bibles or trained priests or basic religious education—is desperately needed." In 1994 the mandate for the office was extended until 1997.

Often working in partnership with other agencies in the United States and Western Europe, the office aimed to improve the pastoral capacity of the Catholic Church in Central and Eastern Europe through aiding the formation of priests and religious; developing catechetical programs, materials, and teachers; providing training, equipment, and funds for mass media communications and charitable work. Among those helped were a Jesuit novitiate and a parish kindergarten in Hungary; victims of family breakdown in Ukraine; and Lithuanian seminarians studying in Rome. Duplicating machinery has done wonders in making religious material available in Magadan on Russia's Pacific coast and in St. Petersburg. Projects to aid the prolife movement and the family were funded in Ukraine, the Czech Republic, and Poland. Social-charitable aid is provided by various national Caritas organizations such as those of the Scandinavians, which help Baltic Catholics, while in France, Belgium, and Italy Catholic organizations independent of Caritas continue the aid that they have given for years.

Needs vary greatly. In October 1991 a bearded Jesuit Georg Sporschill, forty-five, with three lay companions from the Caritas Youth Home of Vienna, set out for Bucharest. He knew some of the needs he would be trying to meet but had little idea how to go about it. He wanted to help Bucharest's street children, products of broken homes or harsh institutions. Many of these unkempt children, often suffering from festering sores, lice-ridden, and sniffing glue from plastic bags, all psychologically impaired, gathered regularly at the Romanian capital's North Railway Station. Sporschill and his companions, using hastily-learned Romanian, first contacted them there.

The Austrian group acquired and cleaned a house where they accommodated twenty street children, then prepared another for thirty, and each afternoon took bread and friendship to those at the station itself. The children appreciated the attention, the new clothes, and regular meals but had to learn to live in a community. Ranging upwards from five years, they received instruction at the homes until ready to attend schools. Romanians were involved in the project, as the aim was eventually to leave it in their hands.

"It reinforces our hope," Sporschill said, "to see the children sometimes trying to outdo each other in making the Sign of the Cross in Latin or Orthodox fashion or any way at all . . . our social work is an ecumenical challenge."

More homes have been acquired in Bucharest and also a rundown fifteen-acre farm fifty miles away towards the Carpathian mountains. Here live drug-damaged children, older ones who lack schooling, and those who want to farm or learn trades such as bread-making, carpentry, or metal work. And at the North Station, where Sporschill first met the members of what threatened to be a lost generation, he opened a social assistance center.

Healing had to be brought also to the Czech regions near the German border. After World War II, even though their forebears had settled there in the thirteenth century, ethnic Germans were expelled from this region. It is said that, as they left, these victims of ethnic cleansing cursed the zone. This, or subsequent government neglect, made it an economic and cultural waste land.

Seventy-five percent of the Catholic population was expelled. Some Catholics arrived among the new settlers, but no churches were built where they lived. The middle generation of inhabitants were mostly atheists, and there were few priests. In other words, it was missionary territory, but mission to economically-depressed, atheistically-indoctrinated, rootless people is daunting. Aid to the Church in Need supplied a chapel van in an attempt to reach young people. The van, thirty-two feet long, has a library, a video with external screens, a sacristy and mobile altar, beds, a living room where confessions can be heard, a galley, shower, and lavatory. Organized by the Dominicans of Prague, it increased youth interest in the Church by visiting summer youth camps and priestless parishes.

Several aid organizations have been involved in supplying Bibles, prayer books, religious literature, and catechetical materials in various forms to ex-Communist Europe. In the five years to 1994, Aid to the Church in Need printed and despatched almost five million religious books to the former Soviet Union and supplied videos and financed religious broadcasts to offset the shortage of priests. Aid to the Church in Need established Radio Blagovest, which began in the late 1980s with three half-hour religious programs weekly beamed from Western Europe; by 1996 it was broadcasting sixteen hours weekly from within the former Soviet Union, including programs requested by the Russian Army, and through the Catholic Radio Veritas in Manila to the former Soviet Asian Republics.

———

The Communist government confiscated the Prague seminary. Among other things, it was used for Warsaw Pact meetings and was also the seat of a Communist publishing house. After its restitution, a grant from Aid to the Church in Need enabled acquisition of the fittings and equipment which had been installed. Now it is not only a seminary but also headquarters of the Czech Bishops' Conference.

But in many countries return of Church property has been exasperatingly slow or incomplete. It is frustrating for Lithuanian Catholics, for instance, to know that they could establish schools if only certain buildings were restituted. In mid 1995, the secretary of the Hungarian Bishops' Conference said that, although guaranteed by parliamentary act in 1991, restitution of church property was "in the deep freeze." But return of property is a complex matter. For one thing, who is to pay for restoring its original condition after others have used it? Often state or local administrations say they have no money to buy it back from later proprietors. Should the Church push for return of buildings now serving a social purpose, such as hospitals? Or should it seek, instead, financial recompense? Catholics do not always agree on what their Church should claim nor whether the battle for property is worth the hostility it can arouse.

The Orthodox have similar problems. The Moscow Patriarchate requested return of all confiscated property, including forests, lakes, icons in the Tretyakov Gallery, and church plate in the Russian Museum. However Father Gleb Jakunin, of the parliamentary Committee for Religious Organizations, rejected the demands as unrealistic, arguing that before 1917 the Church was an arm of the government rather than an independent proprietor and changes in land use had made restitution impossible.

Situations are often more intricate than they first appear. Lithuanian priests who, although without compromising, accepted Communist constraints had a more restful life than when, after Communism's demise, they could engage in a full range of activities. They also found that in the post-Communist era they were poorer because of inflation. Moreover some disliked Archbishop Audrys Bačkis's introduction of parish accounts and transfer from one parish to another. They were used to being barons in their own fiefs. In countries like the United States, parishes usually have basic furniture to which resident priests might add, but many Lithuanian parish priests took everything with them when they transferred. The new policies caused grumbling against Bačkis as a foreigner: born in Vilnius in 1937, he had lived in France, the Vatican (working in the Secretariat of State), and elsewhere. Even the native-born could become suspect if they have spent time in other countries.

Tact is necessary in rebuilding ecclesial communities. Central and Eastern European priests, unfamiliar with the practice of accounting for the use of aid funds, often resent a request to do so. Some of the thirty surviving Catholic priests in Albania were shocked by aspects of Church aid such as foreign priests and sisters eating meals together, aid workers wearing brief shorts in mountain villages, or Italian seminary professors not being able to lecture in Albanian after more than a year in the country.

In a country where until recently windows were opened in summer during surgical operations in hospitals without air conditioning, a Salesian youth center in Shkodër with sports facilities and a video room can seem part of the opulent West. "Certainly that's a danger," admitted an Italian Salesian, Father Renato Toresan; "we want to give the best we can, but at the same time we have to convince youth that the Church means values more durable and worthwhile than opulence."

The Italian Caritas organization, which coordinated all Catholic aid in Albania, played an important role in staving off starvation and also encouraged local initiatives such as new bakeries. Another of these initiatives was improving living conditions within the women's prison of Tiranë and providing work opportunities for inmates, for instance supplying leather which they made into gloves. Sold locally, the gloves gave the prisoners an income. In 1993 Italian Caritas established a corresponding Albanian organization which gradually assumed full responsibility for aid.

Father Zef (Jozef) Pllumi at sixty-nine was the youngest surviving Franciscan after the demise of Communism. Imprisoned for twenty-five years, on release in 1989 he came from his native Shkodër to the capital Tiranë to reclaim St. Anthony's Church. Interviewed there, Zef complained that there had been too little aid too late, adding that there can be too much alleged concern for local sensibilities. As an example of this, he recounted that a deacon and his wife had been working in his parish but a "higher church authority" persuaded them to leave on the grounds that their presence would make local Catholics think the Church now accepted a married priesthood. "People would've recognized he was a deacon," said Zef; "much more use should've been made also of lay ministries—in this the sects were prompter."

In 1994 the Opus Dei movement, which already had houses in Hungary, Slovakia, and the Czech Republic, decided to establish others in Ukraine, Lithuania, Croatia, and Slovenia. Ecclesial groups such as Communione e Liberazione, the Focolare, and the Neocatechumenate have sent members to spread the faith in ex-Communist Europe. Sometimes local Catholics and the traditional religious orders consider the new movements shallow and disruptive. However Father Florian Pełka, the Jesuit president of the Polish Conference of Major Religious Superiors, believes that they enrich religious life and foster vocations. His most intense religious experience, he recounts, came through the Neocatechumenate, and he recommends "dual membership" —that is, members of religious orders participating also in newer movements. But some movements verge on becoming sects, as in the case of extremist Marian groups which appeal to those who believe that they alone preserve a threatened faith.

———

The religious orders' international character should give them a key role in rebuilding the Church in ex-Communist Europe; but in the West, because of the slump in vocations, most have few qualified men and women to spare for Central and Eastern Europe.

The orders' international character was both an advantage and disadvantage during Communism. The advantage was that, as the orders were allowed to continue some public activities in Poland, East Germany, Yugoslavia, and to a small degree in Hungary, clandestine religious from other Communist countries went there for rest and recreation or, rather, for study and an experience of traditional community life. (Vocation figures reflect the considerable differences in conditions. In Poland, for instance, between 1950 and 1990 Franciscans nearly doubled their numbers, 679 to 1,218, while in Yugoslavia they increased from 1,294 to 1,414. But in Lithuania, in the same period, their numbers declined from 128 to only 40, in Romania from 210 to 60, in Hungary from 600 to 195, and in Czechoslovakia from 334 to 137.) The differences between countries persist. In some, the orders have been able to rely on local personnel to rebuild, but in others they have had to turn to outsiders. In Albania, for instance, the three surviving Jesuits have been joined by ten from other countries, and something similar has happened in Romania.

The orders' international character also caused embarrassment at times for those suffering under Communist regimes. Although more than 200 Jesuits were refused permission to function legally in Czechoslovakia, the American Jesuit Daniel Berrigan attended a regime-backed peace conference in Prague. In 1984, the Flemish Dominican Edward Schillebeeckx was keynote speaker in a Prague colloquium on peace. Václav Malý, describing himself as a Catholic priest deprived of a state license, wrote to Schillebeeckx that he "had been unwittingly used . . . by a government that suppresses every spontaneous expression of its citizens' convictions."

If rebuilding is limited to parishes, there is a danger of withdrawing into a ghetto: so said Dominik Duka, head of the Czech Dominicans, when interviewed in a small and shabby room in Prague soon after Communism's demise. The furniture in the room was as old as the books on the shelves, where ping pong paddles peeped from between worse-for-wear theological texts. It was the rectory of a church on Jan Hus Street near Wenceslas Square. After decades, black and white Dominican robes were again visible on Prague streets, but chubby Duka wore black trousers and a pullover. He said that the idea of Europe had been nurtured in monasteries and universities and the Church should again concentrate on them.

The son of a teacher, Duka made his Dominican novitiate clandestinely and was ordained in 1970 at the age of twenty-seven. Although his license as a priest was withdrawn, he continued to celebrate Mass. Discovered, he was sentenced to fifteen months' imprisonment for "obstructing state supervision of Churches." Until January 1990 he worked in the Skoda factory in Pilsen but continued to minister secretly as a Dominican.

Duka said oppression had forced Dominicans to appreciate their faith more, "as it was the only thing which gave us hope. Our situation also gave us a greater appreciation of whatever community life we managed to have, of contemplation, and of prayer such as the Liturgy of the Hours. Our contacts with fellow workers, in factories and elsewhere, which were not possible before, led to solidarity with all those striving for truth, freedom, and equality. Although circumstances have changed, I think we can build on this deeper religious awareness combined with human solidarity." By 1994 he was vice-president of the European Association of Religious Men and Women, who numbered 450,000.

In the Western tradition religious orders are often trailblazers, but this is not so true of the East. "The religious of Ukraine, perhaps because of the influence of Eastern monasticism, are reluctant to make any changes," Cardinal Myroslav Lubachivsky of Lviv told the meeting on the religious life held in the Vatican in October 1994. At the same time he reported that the orders had many recruits: the five male orders, with 407 members, had 120 novices; the eleven female orders had 750 sisters and 127 novices.

Several Central and Eastern European countries look to female orders as the only source of nurses prepared to care for the terminally ill and the mentally handicapped. This has helped some orders reacquire confiscated institutions. For many of these nuns, wearing a religious habit is a conquest, which illustrates the difference from nuns in the West.

Contemplatives are also reestablishing their convents: nuns who suffered deportation, imprisonment, and forced labor have returned to their former abodes in Ukraine, Hungary, and, above all, Czechoslovakia.

The Cistercian convent at Érdliget, twelve miles from Budapest, is a different case, as it functioned clandestinely throughout the Communist era. In 1945 Father Emil, a Hungarian Cistercian monk, was asked to establish the nation's first Cistercian convent and began with eight young novices, who were all still nuns in 1994. They transformed a stable into a convent. In 1949, at the exceptionally young age of nineteen, Gemma Punk became abbess; but the following year the community, like others, was disbanded by government order. The nuns kept in touch with one another and after some time were able to buy a house with grounds on the outskirts of Érdliget, where they reassembled under Father Emil's guidance. They all worked and gradually enlarged the house until it had eight rooms. Every day before praying as a community they closed the doors and windows.

A nun who had been found unsuitable to continue in the community informed the secret police of its existence. The house-convent was turned upside down by the police one day in October 1968. For a month Father Emil and Abbess Punk were questioned daily, but the police could not find anything justifying a charge of secret contacts with state enemies (the charge made against Cardinal Mindszenty in the 1950s). And the neighbors, who now knew that the house's occupants were nuns, spoke well of them.

They were allowed to continue living in the house, which received official recognition as the Regina Mundi Institute in 1989. In 1991 a convent was built on the grounds, and three novices took their first vows. The nuns became involved in catechesis and pastoral work.

―――

Although Catholic schools can now function in most of ex-Communist Europe, limits are posed by the shortage of teachers, textbooks, and buildings, often because states have not given back school buildings they seized or have returned them in a pitiable condition.

Some Communist governments, such as those of Lithuania and Romania, prohibited religious instruction in schools whereas others, such as those of Czechoslovakia and Hungary, allowed it. But it was largely a formal difference, as parents had to request the instruction and this could disadvantage the students concerned. In some countries, such as Poland and East Germany, religious education was allowed in parishes.

In most of ex-Communist Europe, students in state schools choose now between religion and ethics classes, but in September 1994 Romania and Georgia made religion classes obligatory in state schools. At that time in Hungary there were 171 Christian schools (108 of them Catholic), about 3 percent of the total.

In Poland ninety-three Catholic schools had been revived by the beginning of the 1994–95 school year. Moreover, Opole University in Silesia became the first state institution to open its own theology faculty. Expanded Jesuit faculties in Warsaw (theology) and Cracow (philosophy) had many lay students, most of whom would become religious teachers in state schools, and the same was true of the Jesuit philosophy faculty in Zagreb, Croatia. In Lithuania, the Jesuits had revived their former schools in Vilnius and Kaunas. Although their legal status was uncertain, a few Catholic schools were functioning in Albania. At the end of 1994 a Catholic school was inaugurated in Sarajevo, while more than a hundred Catholic schools, funded by the state, were functioning in Slovakia.

In rebuilding ecclesial communities, spiritual retreat houses and seminaries play crucial roles because retreats enable a deepening of spirituality, whose very existence was denied formerly by the prevailing powers, and seminaries provide a thorough training for priests after decades of inevitably sketchy preparation. Many retreat houses have resumed functioning with success, and seminaries are training the first generation of post-Communist priests, whether in Tiranë or at the Jesuit-staffed institute in Shkodër, Albania; at the makeshift seminary in porta-cabins outside the Church of the Immaculate Conception, Moscow; or at the Riga seminary, which taught in Russian when it served the whole Soviet Union but now as a national seminary uses Latvian. The number of seminaries in what had been the Soviet Union increased by 1995 from two to eight. Pioneering work is being done at the seminaries of Lviv (Ukraine) and Grodno (Belarus).

By mid 1993, there were 328 seminarians, 157 of them married men, in the Lviv Eastern-rite seminary, which had only ninety-six rooms for students. The emergency experienced under Communism never ended for Archbishop Sterniuk, who opened Holy Spirit Seminary in 1990 and accepted applicants regardless of their marital status. But from 1994 no married men have been accepted. Students are not free to marry until their final year. Somehow, three priests educated and formed the seminarians. There was no spiritual director. It was better than training-on-the-run, which was all that was possible in the Communist era, but was it good enough? There was virtually no library apart from some theological books in Ukrainian. There was a prejudice against texts in Russian; an attempt was being made to build up holdings of books in German and English.

In 1989 Tadeusz Kondrusiewicz, who had graduated as a hydraulic engineer from Leningrad University before becoming a priest, was made apostolic administrator of Belarus. The first bishop appointed there in sixty-two years, he opened a seminary in his home town, Grodno, where he resided because he was not allowed to live in the capital, Minsk. At the end of World War II, the Soviet Union's frontiers were extended westward to include what had been part of Poland. As a result ethnic Poles constituted the bulk of Belarus's 2.5 million Catholics, but most of their churches had been closed and only protests by the laity managed to keep the remainder open. For instance, only two Masses were allowed yearly in Grodno's baroque cathedral, but the faithful gathered there each Sunday for the Liturgy of the Word. There were only sixty aged priests left in Belarus when Kondrusiewicz was appointed, but he was determined to train young replacements in a former Franciscan monastery which was being used as a hospital. It had a broken roof and damp walls, and all fittings were in poor shape.

The three-story seminary opened in September 1990. It had only one lavatory and one wash room for thirty-eight students and the staff. Under supervision, the students rebuilt the edifice as they studied. By 1993 there were sixty-five students and the unfenced seminary had a gleaming, aluminum-alloy, high-gabled roof, ditches had been dug around the walls to combat the damp, a completely new refectory had been built, and new student rooms had been inserted in the third floor ("this floor is almost European-standard," wryly commented the Polish prefect of studies, Father Roman Kotlimowski).

However six of the ten teaching staff were not resident, having pastoral posts outside Grodno, and the library numbered only 5,000 volumes, most of which were in Polish, as until independence Belarusan was considered a Russian dialect.

"In many cases the faith was transmitted to these students by their grandparents," said Father Kotlimowski when interviewed at the seminary. "They've a thirst for Catholic teaching, but even the most basic theological terms have to be explained to them. We want to ensure a solid spiritual foundation—in Poland, to a large degree, the Catholic faith has already been contaminated."

Something similar was said by Father Andrejs Maria Jerumanis, who had Latvian parents but grew up in Belgium, where he took a medical degree before becoming a priest. "People here are more open to spiritual values than those in the West: they're grateful to the Church for resisting Communism," said Jerumanis, who returned to Latvia at the age of thirty-six when appointed rector of the Riga seminary in 1992. "But young people who look admiringly to the West are very vulnerable. There'll be a few years before Western consumerism corrodes the spiritual interest which accompanied the end of Communism. In these few years we have to infuse Christian values in society."

In Slovakia, where there was only one seminary during the Communist era, there were six by 1993 with 933 seminarians—proportionally six times more than in Belgium. Moreover all dioceses had bishops—some sees had been vacant for forty years—and they initiated a decade-long spiritual renewal program. Many courses for catechetical teachers had been organized to meet the demand for religious teachers in state schools. The Komensky University in Bratislava had inaugurated a theology faculty. Religious orders and lay apostolate groups were expanding. The state had restored some confiscated Church property. In the census, 3.6 of Slovakia's 5.3 million people identified themselves as Catholic.

———

Under Communism, Catholics and many others looked to the pope; after Communism, there were Vatican representatives close at hand. They were a mixed lot. The Vatican diplomatic service was unprepared for its sudden expansion in Central and Eastern Europe. Initially some complained that Vatican representatives in their country did not know the language, but a second group of appointees were better equipped. Those, Catholic or not, who had admired the pope as a paladin of democracy and human rights were disappointed that Vatican diplomats tended to be more cautious on such matters. Some attributed this to continuation of contacts made during the Vatican's *Ostpolitik.*

The diplomats had an important role to play in respect to newly constituted bishops' conferences. But the Council of European Bishops' Conferences, rather than the Vatican, brought their representatives together for the first time, in Warsaw in October 1994, to share insights and even to examine the mistakes made during and after the Communist era. Representatives of the German, Austrian, French, and Italian episcopates also attended the meeting, which was an example of the increasing collaboration between Churches which, under Communism, had been isolated from one another as well as from the West: religious orders, youth and university student organizations (such as Pax Romana), and media groups have begun working together.

The Warsaw meeting prompted reflection about Central and Eastern European bishops, many of whom have had unusual formative experiences in the school of hard knocks, sometimes from prison guards. Often their experiences were what one might expect of novelists rather than bishops. A goodly proportion are unfamiliar with the ways of Church administration but have done manual labor, sometimes in forced-labor camps. Like St. Paul, they sustained themselves by the work of their hands; and, as Cardinal Korec said, they had learned like Paul to "preach only Christ crucified."

Mikel Koliqi, for instance, who had studied engineering in Italy before becoming a priest and then on return to his native Albania had been a composer of opera and liturgical music, choirmaster, poet, and editor of a magazine, was condemned to a total of forty-four years between prisons and labor camps, where he did exhausting work draining swamps. Released at the age of eighty-four, he returned to Shkodër but, when Communism was replaced, was not nominated bishop. However in 1994, John Paul made him, at the age of ninety-two, Albania's first cardinal. He died in January 1997.

Koliqi was the first to admit that he was too old to contribute much to the post-Communist Catholic Church, but Sigitas Tamkevičius, who edited the clandestine *Chronicle of the Catholic Church in Lithuania,* returned at fifty still vigorous after five and a half years in labor camps. He became spiritual director, then rector of the Kaunas seminary. In May 1990 he was made one of Kaunas's two auxiliary bishops with responsibility for the media and catechetics. Apart from Lithuanian, Tamkevičius knows only Russian and a little Polish, but after Communism's collapse he traveled in Italy, France, and Germany. He has said that Lithuanian seminarians want the relaxed style of their Western counterparts but have to accept the responsibility that goes with it. He has welcomed those changes introduced by the Vatican Council which sustain young people's interest in the faith. In May 1996 he succeeded Cardinal Vincentas Sladkevičius as archbishop of Kaunas.

There were still younger bishops (the average age of the Catholic bishops in Bulgaria was forty) who knew nothing other than Communist regimes but had not been in work camps or prisons. Jan Lenga, the apostolic administrator of Kazakhstan, who also had responsibility for Latin-rite Catholics in four other Central Asian Republics (Kirghizstan, Uzbekistan, Turkmenistan, and Tajikistan), was born in Ukraine in 1950 of ethnic Polish parents (his father was a cobbler). He had no formal religious training; but, inspired by a priest he met in his village when he was twenty, felt he had a priestly vocation. After joining the Marian Order in Lithuania, he studied for the priesthood in secret while working to maintain himself there and in Latvia. One day in 1979 he was made a deacon, the next day he was ordained a priest, and the following day left Lithuania to confound anyone on his tracks. He did pastoral work in Dushanbe, Tajikistan, even though he did not know German, the language of most of his parishioners. After six months he was sent to Krasnoarmejsk in Kazakhstan for a month but stayed eleven years until made apostolic administrator responsible for a huge area which had been put under the same jurisdiction for the first time. There were twenty diocesan priests (four of them were members of the Volga-German Messmer family who, as recounted, were influenced by the Lithuanian Jesuit, Albinas Dumbliauskas) and some religious to serve an estimated 500,000 Catholics mainly of German, Polish, Ukrainian, Czech, and Slovak origin.

On appointment, Lenga warned against a tendency to absolutize race, ethnicity, and religion. He favored ethnically mixed parishes with the liturgy celebrated in various languages to show that "it's the Mass which makes Catholics rather than ethnicity." Bishop Lenga, who had no administrative training, no university education or normal parish experience, had to find out by himself how to be a bishop in circumstances unknown outside Kazakhstan. He admitted it has been difficult but discovered under the previous regime that "if one knows who one is and is prepared to take risks, a way can always be found around problems." But he pointed out that

Kazakhstan, which is twelve times larger than Poland, has only 1 bishop and 32 priests whereas Poland has 111 bishops and 27,000 priests; he has deplored the fact that because of the difficult conditions more Polish priests do not come to Kazakhstan.

On being appointed bishop in 1991, slightly-built Joseph Werth had only two priests (one of them Józef Świdnicki, the man who had studied theology perched in a crane in Riga) for all of Siberia; but in four years he attracted another fifty-three from many countries, including India and the United States.

Werth was born in 1952 in Karaganda, Kazakhstan, of deported Volga Germans; while doing his compulsory military service, he had read an antireligious text which derided the Jesuits. This whetted his interest. In Lithuania he contacted some Jesuits and began a clandestine novitiate with them even before entering the Kaunas seminary. Ordained in 1984, he was doing pastoral work at Marx (his first language is Russian) when nominated apostolic administrator of Siberia, where it is estimated that there are 100,000–150,000 Catholics in a territory larger than the United States. They have found each other partly through radio, newspaper, and television advertisements. Werth's secretary was Aleksandr Kahn, whose story has already been told; the first priest Werth ordained was Joseph Messmer, whose five brothers are priests and whose three sisters are nuns, as is his widowed mother.

In Siberia, by 1995 sixty churches had been reactivated, including the Cathedral of the Most Holy Mother of God in the Pacific seaport of Vladivostok. There and elsewhere Catholics were engaged in development projects with non-Catholics; construction of the Transfiguration Cathedral, whose cornerstone is from near St. Peter's tomb in Rome, was underway in Novosibirsk, where Jesuits were teaching at the state university and the teachers' college and were also running a Center for Culture and Spirituality. A small seminary had been opened and a monthly Catholic paper established. At the end of 1994, fifty-five priests, sixty nuns, and seventy-five lay parish representatives attended the first Siberian pastoral conference in Novosibirsk.

Miloslav Vlk, who presided over the bishops' meeting in Warsaw, was perhaps the most internationally prominent of those promoted swiftly after the fall of Communism. He had washed windows in Prague for eight years after Communist authorities withdrew his license to function as a priest but, at the beginning of 1989, was allowed to resume his priestly ministry in a village where there was not even a telephone. Early in 1990 he was made bishop of a diocese with 850,000 inhabitants and, the following year, was appointed successor to Cardinal František Tomášek as archbishop of Prague and primate of Bohemia. Previously he had lived in cramped quarters; now he moved into an historic residence with Gobelin tapestries. After Communism's demise, aided by his knowledge of many languages, Vlk rapidly caught up with developments in the West. He said it made him realize that although Western theologians had a bad reputation in the East only a few deserved it. In 1993 he became president of the Council of European Bishops' Conferences and, in November 1994, a cardinal. It was as president of the Council of European Bishops' Conferences that he presided over the Warsaw meeting.

As Vlk and other Central European bishops had seen that hostile authorities aimed to split the Church, it is not surprising that they are more accustomed to cleaning windows than opening them as did John XXIII. But they have also found that many Church structures are dispensable, which makes them, in some respects, surprisingly free. Because they were forced to take humble jobs or share prison cells they tend to be self-reliant, have the common touch, and trust the laity. They consider religious rights the basis for all other human rights. Above all, they have seen that Christianity generates great dynamism if only its potential can be released.

Vlk invited the participants at the Warsaw meeting to "soberly assess" Catholic policies and behavior under Communism and after it. Another Czech, Father Tomáš Halík, who had been secretary to the bishops' conference but was now president of the Prague Christian Academy, soberly said that after Communism crumbled the Catholic Church had made a mistake by losing touch with intellectuals.

Even though in Poland, as in Yugoslavia and East Germany, the Catholic Church under Communism maintained many of its structures, Bishop Tadeusz Pieroñek, secretary of the Polish Bishops' Conference, complained that Christians had acquired a ghetto mentality which would last until they participated in pastoral-social work. Indeed the need to overcome the privatization of religion induced by Communism became one of the themes of the Warsaw meeting. Such privatization was overcome temporarily in the protests which preceded Communism's collapse, but several participants observed that Christians no longer connected their beliefs with their social life. It was not easy, even for bishops' conferences or individual bishops, to find the proper relationship to social issues: for instance, Archbishop Audrys Bačkis of Vilnius avoided Catholic Church involvement in party politics, but some local Catholics, who were not necessarily diehards, would have liked him to state more forcefully Catholic social teaching.

Rebuilding ecclesial communities will take longer than many had imagined. Only in 1996 did the first priests trained wholly in the post-Communist era come into parishes; for many religious order priests, who train longer, the date will be about 2000. The first post-Communist generation will not become adult until 2010. At least the Warsaw meeting showed that bishops' conferences were beginning to face together some Church problems; but those of society, where increasingly dubious characters prospered and it seemed the devil would take the hindmost, were taking a new form.

Chapter 12

The Happiest Day and After

The happiest day after the fall of a tyrant is the first.
Tacitus, Histories 4.42.6

In Communist Europe, there was a healthy reaction against stifling constraints, fear, and boredom. People wanted to hear the truth but also to break rules. Some sought meaning in the faith or in cultural pursuits; others sought anything flashy to liven the greyness. Western cars seemed chariots of fire. Rock music stood for an anarchic wildness and energy, an attempt to break through to the other side. Indeed Václav Havel has attributed his involvement in the protest movement to it: he considers that Lou Reed's Velvet Underground influenced the Velvet Revolution. He has recounted that organizing support for a banned Czech rock group, Plastic People of the Universe, was one of the origins of the Charter 77 movement. After Communism's collapse, Havel sought the advice of Frank Zappa of the duster moustache, miniature goatee, and aquiline nose, the founder of the Mothers of Invention and of the Honker Home Video Company, on the creation of enterprise culture. Who knows in what order of importance Havel graded his invitations to Czechoslovakia: Zappa; the latest reincarnation of the Bodhisattva of Compassion, the Dalai Lama (also known as the Ocean of Wisdom); and John Paul II?

The years of opposition to Communism were years of high moral seriousness, of weighty discussions, of courageous resolve. With Communism's demise, people were able to act as well as discuss. Church attendances dropped as did interest in books, classical concerts, stage plays, and other cultural activities. As a Polish publisher said, people simply wanted to let their hair down and stuff their faces.

Some, such as the former Polish Communist government spokesman Jerzy Urban, who founded a satiric-pornographic magazine, claimed emergent pornography was an expression of freedom. He might have been at least partly right if he had advanced the argument at the time of the Communist government; but, while its spokesman, he was silent on this issue. Communist regimes were an odd mixture of inefficiency and imposed shortages. Scarcity seemed programed as salutary. One deprivation was of beauty and sensuousness, which, for these utilitarian regimes, were superfluous. From clothing to food to architecture, Communist societies starved the senses. They denied sexuality too and wanted to control it as potentially subversive. Sexuality served to produce workers, but the regimes tried to make it invisible.

In this context, girlie magazines could be understood as a protest, an attempt to reassert what was denied. Unfortunately, deprivation made the deprived grasp at crude versions of what they were missing. It makes them vulnerable today to exploiters, many of them from Western Europe; but it would be mistaken for Central and Eastern European Christians to think that these exploiters represent all the West and to ignore the background to this hunger.

In the controlled Central and Eastern European press, pornography, like drug abuse, was deplored as a Western blight. But Communist regimes also laid the grounds for consumerism, because they claimed to have mastered economic matters but did not deliver the goods. In a sense, the events of 1989 were a revolution of falling expectations: people despaired of ever closing the gap with the West unless the regimes changed.

"Consumerism" is used to cover a multitude of sins. John Paul II fears it will undermine social solidarity. A consumerist society knows the price of everything and the value of nothing; it tends to live beyond its means. At its worst, it becomes the antithesis of a sacramental sense of life. But East Germans who had no choice but to buy, after a long wait, primitive Trabant cars would have welcomed consumerist choice. Central and Eastern Europeans gawking at Western tourists' cars epitomized deprivation. In the Soviet Union, even light bulbs became precious. So did fruit: in much of Communist Europe oranges were a treasure and fruit salad an unimaginable luxury.

On his fourth Polish visit John Paul II claimed that materialism is "more consolidated" in Western than Eastern Europe, but a Polish Jesuit noted "nothing is worse than our consumerism of desire." It is not surprising that those thwarted by an unsuccessful materialism should envy the West, particularly when they often have naive ideas about the extent of Western affluence.

John Paul uses "consumerism" to include all forms of hedonism, of practical atheism. But it has a more specific meaning and in this sense can be best combated by measures to protect consumers and to ensure that business people observe rules. Probably people just have to find their way beyond consumerism; Christians who practice detachment can usefully point the way.

Exclusive ethnicity and narrow nationalism are also temptations for Central and Eastern European Christians. Christianity has championed Europe's nondominant groups, often against nation-states, preserving ethnic cultures which enshrined religious values. Catholic, Orthodox, and Protestant Churches have promoted ethnic groups' language, literature, and traditions.

The Sorbs, a Slavic group numbering about 70,000 in southeast Germany, provide an intriguing example of the Catholic Church's defense of minority cultures. The Sorbs have never achieved statehood, but their language and customs have been nurtured by the Church. Catholicism has played a vital role in reinforcing the identity of other Central and Eastern European peoples, such as the Albanians and Lithuanians, but it has balanced the romantic notion of indigenous culture as the "imprint of the people's soul" with awareness of Christianity's shared inheritance.

There have been horrendous examples of nationalistic Catholic regimes such as those of Ante Pavelic in Croatia and Monsignor Jozef Tiso in Slovakia during World War II. Some Slovaks still look to Tiso, who governed from 1938 to 1945, as a patriot and want a revision of the historical judgement on him. Undoubtedly he was a zealous nationalist, but his regime was also one of Europe's most anti-Semitic. In July 1990 a memorial plaque to him as the founder of the first independent Slovak Teacher Training College was unveiled in the town of Bánovce nad Bebravou but, after protests, was removed.

Slovakia, which had been under Hungarian rule for centuries, was yoked together with Bohemia, Moravia, and Transcarpathian Ruthenia to form Czechoslovakia after World War I. The more prosperous and educated Czechs dominated the new state. Slovaks resented the Prague government, which they considered too secular. When, in 1939, the Nazis invaded the Czech lands, Hitler agreed to the creation of a pro-German Slovak Republic with Tiso as president. Tiso imposed a censorious, autocratic Catholic rule, outlawed the smaller Churches but not Protestantism, and promoted Slovak language and culture at the expense of other ethnic groups. Without prompting, Slovakia deported 58,000 out of a total of 90,000 Jews to German concentration camps. Tiso's supporters claim it was believed they were going to work camps in Poland. In 1943, under pressure from the Vatican, Tiso suspended deportations and in his own church read out the condemnation of them which the Slovakian Catholic bishops had finally issued.

Tiso's government, which had not won a majority in a free election, was swept aside in 1945. In Bratislava two years later, he was executed as a war criminal. In an underground publication in 1987, twenty-four Slovaks, half of them Christians, begged forgiveness for Tiso's anti-Semitism. One of the signatories was Ján Korec, now a cardinal, but he attended the unveiling of the Teachers' College plaque to Tiso.

More recently, Archbishop Julijonas Steponavičius of Vilnius, who died in mid 1991, refused to allow Poles a symbolic Mass in the Vilnius cathedral or Polish priests to fill gaps in the Lithuanian clergy. It was a response to Polish discrimination against Lithuanians that Steponavičius had suffered as a young priest, but it revealed pettiness in a courageous nationalist.

The Vatican Council, with its condemnation of anti-Semitism and abandonment of the idea of a Catholic state, has made clerical-fascist states less likely in Central and Eastern Europe. But it was a startling novelty to have a pope, John Paul II, who worked the nationalist seam. In recent Western European history, several nation-states were formed against the Catholic Church; Italy is a prime example. Interestingly enough, there was a strong tradition of recruiting the Holy See's diplomats from the former Papal States on the grounds that they had a Catholic, rather than nationalist, outlook. John Paul's immediate predecessors, although recognizably Italian, were not nationalistic. But he was a patriot demanding, successfully, that Poland's full sovereignty be recognized. He had an acute sense of the difference between a people and a state and did not want to see the richness of peoples' culture and history smothered by the thin gruel of Soviet internationalism. And it must be recognized that the Solidarity movement he encouraged eschewed violence.

But the principle that a people's aspirations must be satisfied seemed to obey the law of diminishing returns. Or, rather, of increasing chaos. As the Communist sphere broke up, some peoples' deepest aspiration seemed to be to slay members of other ethnic groups. It was all very well for the Churches to defend ethnic groups within a state, but what if each ethnic group insisted on forming its own state? Italy had been forged by fighting the Papal States, but when the Lombard League leader, Umberto Bossi, proposed a separate northern Italian state, Italian bishops blew the whistle.

John Paul himself seemed to have second thoughts after the Holy See had quickly recognized the independence of Slovenia, Croatia, and Bosnia, saying that, in the light of the carnage, it might have been better to persist with the idea of a Yugoslav federation which he had proposed when the problem first emerged.

It is not sufficient to condemn everyone's nationalism but one's own, and nationalists are not destined to repeat yesterday's errors. The Ukrainian Rukh movement, for instance, is explicitly tolerant of other ethnic groups. The Ukrainian Youth for Christ movement, in a country where interdenominational strife is endemic, encourages youth to collaborate on social problems across denominational barriers. They do so for Christ's sake but also for the nation's. People can be inspired by a love for their homeland; nationalism is not necessarily the last resort of scoundrels. For instance, nationalist sentiments helped Slovenian Communists to go beyond sectarianism although they were not so beneficial elsewhere in ex-Yugoslavia.

The Orthodox Churches' customary alliance with civil authorities limited their traditional national character during the *pax sovietica*. When it no longer existed they were free to encourage nationalism, which is one of their temptations. Recent Catholic support for people's aspirations is now counterbalanced by underlining the need for social cohesion. The

Churches have always said that a people's legitimate aspirations must be supported, but it is an acute task of discernment to decide on legitimacy. Christendom once supplied people with a larger context, but nowadays it must be substituted by the idea and reality of Europe. In this process the Churches can be a guide, provided they are not themselves blinded by nationalism. The next martyr in post-Communist Europe could be someone courageous enough to go against the narrow nationalism of his or her fellow citizens.

Chapter 13

Justice is not Enough

Justice is not enough . . . it can even lead to the negation and destruction of itself if that deeper power, which is love, is not allowed to shape human life in its various dimensions.

John Paul II, Dives in misericordia, 12

Some in ex-Communist Europe forget the Communist past too readily; others find difficulty in coming to terms with it. If buried, it festers; if faced, it can overwhelm. People were material for grotesque social experiments, deported en masse, buried in secret graveyards which every now and again come to light. Fear drifted in the air. Now daunting questions linger: why did all this happen and where does it leave the survivors?

A regime which used hatred as its social dynamic left a devastating heritage. The internal security services fought the Communists' war against society, and their archives are congealed phials of hatred. Some want them made public, claiming a right to know who spied on them. Others are loath to open them because their half-truths and inventions served only their compilers. Bishop Christopher Demke, as chair of the East German Protestant Church Federation, advised people not to believe blindly the internal security forces' (Stasi) files. "If we want a new beginning," he said, "we must take the risk of trusting our experience and personal insight as the basis for assessing people."

Czech President Václav Havel said that illegal publication of lists of security service collaborators, which included many non-collaborators' names, led to countless tragedies. He approved a de-Communistation provision which excluded former security service personnel above a certain level from the state administration. Havel commented later that it served no practical purpose, as those concerned would have become wealthy entrepreneurs, but it was psychologically useful, as it made people feel they had evened scores with the security services.

There was nothing comparable to Germany's postwar de-Nazification process. Czechoslovakia proscribed security agents. In Poland the names of parliamentarians who had collaborated began to be released but this process was seen as a weapon in the political struggle and was suspended. In East Germany people were able to consult security files to see who had spied on them: some spouses were shocked to find it had been their partner. In Albania some former Communist leaders, such as Nexhmi Hoxha, wife of the former president, were imprisoned. But in several countries no measures were taken at all.

It was not easy to put paid to the Communist past. The case of Erich Honecker, who supervised the building of the Berlin Wall and later led East Germany for eighteen years until 1989, showed its complexities. Honecker, accused among other things of ordering the shooting of those who tried to escape over the Wall, was snatched out of the hands of German justice by Gorbachev as if the doctrine of limited sovereignty still applied. Gorbachev claimed humanitarian motives, pointing out that Honecker was old and sick and had been imprisoned by the Nazis. If Honecker is to be judged, he added, all former Communist leaders could be put on trial instead of being pensioned off. He suggested that a trial of Honecker would be mere vendetta and claimed that the Soviets had forgiven the Germans who had fought for Hitler. But the Soviet Union participated both in the Nuremberg trials and in the division of

Germany for forty-four years. Honecker later returned to Germany, but for health reasons his trial was suspended and he was able to leave for Chile where he died of liver cancer at eighty-one in May 1994. But the questions his case raised abide. If he was not tried, people in Central and Eastern Europe could well ask if anyone was ever to be held responsible. His case illustrates how difficult it is to attain justice.

Doina Cornea, the Romanian university teacher who was dismissed because she insisted that students should seek truth, was bitterly disillusioned by her country's first post-Communist government, which she accused of continuing the previous regime's "moral genocide." (This first post-Communist government was replaced in November 1996 when it seemed the true post-Communist era might begin.) President Nicolae Ceauşescu's immediate successors recommended wiping a sponge over the past. Cornea protested that "forgiving and forgetting cannot be undertaken by the state . . . With an oily, demagogic language those in power try to obtain from us this kind of pardon. It merely increases the moral confusion of people who are already confused and shows how distant [this pardon is] from the Christian spirit."

Perhaps she had in mind cases such as that of Radu Tinu, who in 1992 founded two successful import-export companies. Born in 1946, Tinu joined the Party in his twenties. By age thirty-four he was a major in the Securitate and shortly after became deputy internal security chief for the Timiş Province, the richest in Romania, supervising counterintelligence and disinformation. In late 1989 he directed surveillance of Laszlo Tökes, a Reformed pastor and human rights campaigner. After the pastor ignored an eviction order in 1989, a clash between his supporters, police, and Securitate agents sparked demonstrations, even in Bucharest. All told, more than a hundred people were killed during subsequent clashes, which were the most violent in Central and Eastern Europe; but in the end, Ceauşescu was ousted.

By September 1994 all former Communists had been released from Romanian prisons. Tinu had been accused of ordering Securitate agents to open fire on unarmed protestors, but in 1991 a court of former Communists decided there was insufficient evidence to convict him of first-degree murder. Dapper Tinu, a wine connoisseur, has his import-export office on Timişoara Opera House Square, where thousands of demonstrators gathered in 1989. He has never had it so good.

Whether or not Doina Cornea had in mind cases such as Tinu's, her comments on forgiving and forgetting were a useful reminder that Christian pardon is not simply pretending crimes did not take place. Nor can it be granted by the heirs or successors of the perpetrators, but only by the victims or their relatives. Christian pardon is not an excuse that exonerates from the search for justice; rather it is something of a different order that can benefit the political realm if not confused with it.

Seeking pardon and granting pardon are essential for the reconciliation which can break Communist Europe's heritage of hatred. Grzegorz Piotrowski, the killer of the Solidarity priest Father Jerzy Popiełuszko, sought pardon from the priest's relatives. In 1984, with other members of the Polish secret police, Piotrowski kidnapped Popiełuszko and beat him to death. In 1985 he was condemned to twenty-five years' imprisonment. After a series of meetings with a Catholic journalist, he began to change his outlook and wrote to Popiełuszko's family, which sent him a copy of the sermon Father Jerzy had preached on the night Piotrowski killed him. It concluded with a prayer to be "free from hate and intimidation but most of all from the desire for violence and revenge." Piotrowski commented that Popiełuszko had seen the dangers of yielding to hatred as he (Piotrowski) had done. In 1994, Piotrowski was released from prison.

In postwar Europe there have been many important gestures of reconciliation such as Willy Brandt kneeling in the

Warsaw ghetto to seek pardon for Germany's wartime crimes; German authorities requesting pardon from the Jewish people and financially compensating survivors of the concentration camps; meetings of the German and Polish episcopates to improve relations between their peoples; and the Polish primate, Cardinal Glemp, offering a metaphoric olive branch to the Russians. President Václav Havel wrote to the German President Richard von Weizsäcker asking pardon for the sufferings inflicted on Sudetenland Germans who were driven out of Czechoslovakia after World War II. Discussing his letter in an interview with Adam Michnik, Havel called these expulsions "belated vendetta" and compared postwar anti-German nastiness with current anti-Communist sentiments.

Havel said that as the Czech nation could not be built on lies, errors, or mental stereotypes he tried to touch on matters veiled by forgetfulness, prejudice, or smugness. During World War II, he continued, there were courageous partisans but thousands more collaborators; as a whole, the population did not identify with the partisans any more than it did with dissidents during the 1970s and 1980s.

"But after World War II, thousands of self-proclaimed partisans emerged," Havel continued. "Each underlined his or her merits, was vindictive towards residents of German origin (even innocent people), put on Red Guard armbands, and adorned themselves with medals. Obviously the Communists took advantage of this to gain the allegiance of many with sins on their conscience and of former Gestapo agents whom they used as spies. Society's incapacity to oppose evil and the consequent humiliation means that once evil is defeated belated vendettas are exacted. That's how it was after the war—and how it is now as regards Communism: the most vengeful are those who had sinned themselves. Peoples don't like to hear these things, but I think one must talk of them as they are good for society's mental health. One cannot build an identity on a false foundation, but at the same time one cannot talk of return of property to the Sudetenland Germans and the reparation of all history. As history is full of injustices, of wrongs and expropriated property, there would never be an end to claims."

Havel conveyed the complexity of the situation and the psychological mechanisms which made it easy to confuse justice with vendetta. He also made it clear why many of those who openly resisted Communism were less worried about their former opponents than about the spite, opportunism, and intolerance that have emerged among those who neither were Communists nor opposed them.

Slovenia provided a significant example of a collective attempt to exorcise the past, to dissolve guilt not through juridical procedures but through a reconciliation ceremony. For forty-five years, access to a forest south of Ljubljana was forbidden because it contained evidence of the Communist regime's most heinous crime; in the many fissures in the limestone outcrops were the remains of thousands of postwar victims of Tito's Partisans. In the praying crowd which gathered there in mid 1990 were Communists as well as relatives of the victims.

In 1943, northeastern Slovenia was made a province of Germany (southern Slovenia was under Italian control). As it had been part of the Austro-Hungarian Empire until World War I, it did not find German control wholly uncongenial, particularly as Slovenians were left largely to their own devices. A civil war was raging between Tito's Partisans and groups of anti-Communists who formed a Home Defense (*Domobranci*). At the war's outbreak, 95 percent of Slovenians were Catholic. The majority of *Domobranci* simply wanted to defend their families and homes from the Communists. They had German backing, but many hoped for an Allied victory.

When the Partisans won, the *Domobranci* fled to Austria, which the Allies had liberated. A few months after the end of the war, the British, telling the refugees that they were being sent to safety in Italy, handed them over to the Partisans and certain death. Some were probably war criminals, but there were no trials to ascertain which. Men of fighting age, but also women, children, and the old, perhaps 20,000 in all, were massacred. Most, tied in pairs, were machine-gunned.

Milovan Djilas, a member of the Yugoslav government at the time, has said: "We didn't at all understand why the British insisted on returning these people . . . I ascribe it to the rule of tidy-minded bureaucrats who wanted to clear their desks and close the files. Imbecility . . . the British did completely the wrong thing . . . these killings were senseless acts of wrathful revenge."

The corpses were hidden in the caves at Kočevski Rog, thirty miles south of Ljubljana, along with thousands of Croatian and Serbian victims. Some put the total figure at 30,000. The zone was decreed off-limits. Word of it did not leak out for more than a generation. When it did, there were revelations about seventy other mass graves of victims of the Partisans killed between June and October 1945; it seemed Slovenia was a vast necropolis.

In the 1970s some Slovenians asked publicly why there had been indiscriminate slaughter, why the regime had feared any opposition, who was responsible, and was there any way to reconcile the descendants of the killers with those of the victims.

Spomenka Hribar, the daughter of a Serb married to a Slovenian Communist, learned about the slaughter when she read an interview with the poet Eduard Kocbek. Hribar, who was not a Christian, was to become the leading figure in the reconciliation campaign. But when she broached the subject in the Party she was considered a counterrevolutionary and was made to feel, as she wrote, "homeless in her own country." She was expelled for proposing the construction of a monument to all those who died in the fight between various Slovenian groups. Her proposal was heresy for a party which claimed to be the vanguard of the proletariat and, therefore, the only legitimate representatives of the people. If any opposed it they were counterrevolutionaries, fascists, vermin to be eliminated. To suggest, as had Spomenka Hribar, that all the dead were worthy of commemoration was to subvert this division between the just and unjust. But Hribar joined with others who wanted to lance the abscess. The archbishop of Ljubljana, Alojzij Šuštar, favored commemoration of the victims. Some suggested this could open old wounds and foster new hate. Finally, an open-air ceremony of reconciliation, involving Communists, ex-Communists, and heirs of the victims, was arranged.

On an almost cloudless midsummer morning, July 8, 1990, 30,000 people walked six miles from the nearest township to the site. On the outskirts of the woods they passed a recently erected cross inscribed "Tudi mi smo umrli za domovino" (We too died for the fatherland). In front of the cave with the most (4,000) remains, Pod Krenom, Archbishop Šuštar concelebrated Mass with seventy-five priests, many of whom were relatives of the victims. Prominent in the congregation were the president of Slovenia, Milan Kučan, who had been elected after clashing with Belgrade Communists on the independence issue, and the president of the Slovenian parliament, France Bučar, a law professor who had dared question the legitimacy of the post–World War II incorporation of Slovenia into Yugoslavia without a free vote on the issue.

"In this place of death and mortal silence, of the denial of what was done here, in this place to which access was for long forbidden, today we celebrate the symbolic burial of the *Domobranci* who died here or elsewhere," said Archbishop Šuštar, in his homily. "With this symbolic funeral and Mass, they find again their place and rank in the Slovenian community of the living and the dead." He stressed the need for mutual pardon.

The reconciliation ceremony, said President Kučan in a speech after the Mass, "should have taken place before . . . Reconciliation with all the war's victims is necessary for reconciliation among the living. We sincerely regret what happened."

It was the first time in Slovenia that a Communist had expressed regret in public for the massacres by the Partisans. Šuštar later commented that achieving reconciliation among the living was far more exacting. But at least the Slovenians were on the right path.

The ceremony shows that the wounds of history can be healed, but the victims, or those who stand for them, have to have their say. They cannot give facile forgiveness: those responsible for the crimes have to ask pardon; and usually patience is needed before they become ready to do this, probably because they have to find an ideal which enables them to see their fellowship with the victims.

Killing fields are still being discovered in ex-Communist Europe. In late 1994 mass graves were found in a park on the outskirts of Vilnius. In the early 1950s Soviet security services had secretly killed and buried there hundreds of resistance fighters who opposed the Soviet annexation of Lithuania; the burials continued up to 1953.

One of the most infamous killing fields was in the Katyń Forest, near Smolensk in western Russia. In 1940 approximately a third of the almost 15,000 Polish officers held in Soviet prison camps were secretly murdered in the Katyń Forest. On September 1, 1939, Germany had invaded Poland and the army retreated eastward, but on September 17 the Soviets had invaded also. The Soviets captured Polish officers, imprisoned them, and eventually murdered them to discourage later Polish resistance. When the invading German army later discovered the site in 1943, the Soviets said that the Nazis were responsible for the massacre, but the Poles did not believe them. In 1989 the Soviet Union finally admitted responsibility. The bodies of the other 9,300 officers were found in graves at Mednoye and near

Kharkiv in Ukraine. Moscow allocated funds for exhumation of the remains. In September 1994 the Russian premier, Viktor Chernomyrdin, during a visit to the Katyń Forest site, backed plans for a memorial there to all victims of Communism.

Father Zdzisław Peszkowski, a survivor of the massacre, gave Chernomyrdin an "Act of Unconditional Forgiveness" drawn up by the Katyń Families' Association. Chernomyrdin promised to ensure the return of a confiscated Catholic church in Smolensk to serve as a pilgrimage center for those visiting the sanctuary of reconciliation planned for the site. A Mass for Polish-Russian reconciliation was also celebrated.

Christians initiated reconciliation at Katyń Forest. In the case of what some call the "Slovenian Katyń Forest," Pod Krenom, where the Christians joined in the reconciliation initiated by Spomenka Hribar, who was not a Christian, Archbishop Šuštar encouraged the attempt to heal wounds and provided the form in which it acquired resonance. Christians' familiarity with the sacrament of reconciliation should give them insight into the spiritual dynamic of a process which is essential to opening up a future free from guilt and resentment.

Chapter 14

"Man is Greater than Man"

[One day totalitarianism will] simply disappear, leaving no other trace in the history of mankind than exhausted peoples, economic and social chaos, a political vacuum and a spiritual tabula rasa.

Hannah Arendt, The Origins of Totalitarianism

In St. Petersburg, patriarchs now celebrate the liturgy in the nineteenth-century Orthodox Cathedral of St. Isaac, which until 1989 was a museum of science, with Foucault's pendulum and other instruments to prove that superstition had been defeated and the heavens were empty. The Blood of the Savior Church, whose multicolored bulb domes are mirrored in the nearby canal, has been refurbished; sometimes musicians play brass instruments outside the main door to raise money for its maintenance. The Our Lady of Kazan Church on the Nevsky Prospekt, approached through a semicircular colonnade somewhat like that of St. Peter's in Rome, still has a Museum of Atheism and Religion, but now liturgies are held there also.

Not only Orthodox churches have benefited from the collapse of Communism. On the Nevsky Prospekt alone, within a mile of one another, the Lutheran church, in which a swimming pool was installed, has been restored to the Lutherans; the Armenian Apostolic church, which was used as a storeroom, has been reopened for the city's 15,000 Armenians; and a Catholic church, the largest in Russia, has also been

211

reopened. Two Polish Dominican priests and a French one serve there, while four Italian Dominican nuns aid the parish and plan to open a school. All three churches are called St. Catherine, probably because Czarina Catherine the Great, although no saint, tolerated non-Orthodox denominations.

A walk along the Prospekt is a walk through the history of Christianity. The first splitaways, in the fifth century, were those who did not accept that Christ had a fully human and a fully divine nature; the Armenian Apostolic Church is one example of these so-called Monophysites, who claimed Christ had only one nature. According to the Orthodox, the Catholics split away in the eleventh century because of a Trinitarian controversy; then, in the sixteenth century, the Protestants, represented on the Prospekt by the Lutheran church, followed the Catholic example.

Moscow likewise has striking examples of churches reopened, restored, or being rebuilt. In 1662 it was said that Moscow had forty churches in each of its forty districts. Towards the end of the Communist regime, only a few were functioning. By the beginning of 1995, several hundred were in use. Again Moscow offered the spectacle, as the novelist Joseph Roth had described it before the churches were destroyed, of "golden bulbs, fruit of an exotic, multicolored and bizarre Christianity." On Red Square, St. Basil's, whose architects were blinded by Czar Ivan the Terrible so they would never plan another church to rival its beauty, has been reopened, while the Kazan Cathedral, which celebrated victory over the Poles in 1612, has been rebuilt.

Christ the Savior Church, built between the Kremlin and the Moscow River to celebrate the defeat of Napoleon, who had occupied the city, has been reconstructed in all its kitschy splendor. Consecrated in May 1883 after forty-five years' work, it could accommodate over 10,000 worshippers.

In 1931 Stalin decided to build the Palace of the Soviets where Christ the Savior Church stood. First the demolishers carried away almost half a ton of gold, silver, brass, and bronze (the main bell weighed 24 tons and the twelve gates 140 tons), enamels, precious stones, still more precious icons, and liturgical vestments. It took weeks to prise the marble from the walls. Ryszard Kapuściński, who recounted the demolition in *Imperium,* remarked that this must have irritated Stalin, who at the same time was busy "directing the campaign of killing ten million people in the Ukraine by starvation" and "keeping close watch on the ambitious expansion of the network of labor camps."

The wreckers tried to hammer to smithereens the building that was 325 feet high with walls 10 feet thick but eventually resorted to dynamite. Two years later, in 1933, Stalin approved for the site a construction which was to be six times more massive than the Empire State Building, crowned by a statue of Lenin three times higher and two and a half times heavier than the Statue of Liberty. It would show which was the world's leading power and also be a temple of the new religion whose god was Stalin. But he then became occupied with massacring his opponents through the purge trials, annexing the countries on the Soviet Union's western frontier, fighting the German invaders, deporting whole peoples such as the Chechens and Tartars, whom he suspected of treason, while protecting himself from possible traitors closer at hand by killing them.

Meanwhile, the cathedral site had filled with water where boys fished, frogs croaked, and duckweed proliferated. Drunks and prostitutes took advantage of the abandoned site which, when the fence had been dismantled to make wood fires, became a rubbish dump.

Finally Nikita Khrushchev had the city's largest heated open-air swimming pool installed there. After the demise of Communism, New York interests planned for the site a thirty-story glass and steel tower that would include both a casino and an all-purpose chapel. Now Christ the Savior Church has been rebuilt there. The Russian Orthodox Church has made a point, although some of its members would have preferred to spend the $200 million it cost on restoring derelict provincial churches.

Although churches have taken a new lease of life, much was disquieting five years after the fall of the Wall: in St. Petersburg the streetcars were even more battered than before, the handsome pastel-toned buildings shabbier. Late at night old women lingered in the streets trying to sell single packets of foreign cigarettes. University lecturers eked out a living on forty dollars a month, which had been barely adequate even when rents were frozen. Like other state employees, pensioners, and all those on fixed income, they suffered cruelly from rapid inflation but could see others profiting hugely. People of all ages stood at the exits of pedestrian underpasses selling their pet animals: it was kinder to sell them than to eat them.

In Kiev, desperation was even more patent. It had once been a pleasant stroll along Kiev's stately main thoroughfare, the Avenue of the Friendship of Nations, with its interesting mix of architectural styles including much art nouveau. But five years after the good news about the Wall, the avenue was distressing, lined with women of all ages and conditions holding pieces of cardboard inscribed with dollar signs. If they could get their hands on a dollar they knew it would be worth more the next day. The visitor, with more dollars in one's pocket than a local would earn in a decade, felt like a tempting target.

Although Ukraine has coal mines and a fertile soil, its currency, the karbonavet, made even the ruble look strong, as its rulers tried to solve economic problems simply by printing banknotes. Towards the end of 1994, because suitcases of banknotes were needed to buy even a few goods, the government decided to recycle the smaller karbonavet notes as toilet paper, whose blue, green, and pink tones indicate its origin.

It may have been no coincidence that it was in Kiev that thousands of followers of Marina Tsvygun gathered in November 1993 to witness her crucifixion and await her resurrection three days later. It was to take place before the historic St. Sophia Cathedral, but her followers clashed there with police, damaging eleventh-century icons. Over seven hundred, including Marina, were arrested.

In her posters, Marina wore a long white robe and her white hair was wound above her head like a cotton wig. Her expression was mild, and she held a crosier in her left hand while the first two fingers of the right were raised in blessing, as was appropriate for a messiah. Critics called her sinister. Her pseudonym, Maria Davi Kristos, suggested an Indian goddess as well as the deified virgin who is the messiah. She was a leader of the White Brotherhood, one of a plethora of sects both indigenous and foreign whose popularity reflected the shift.

For many, the concatenation of the collapse of Communism, the end of the empire, and the disintegration of the Soviet Union, followed by economic decline and deterioration of services, have been overly stressful. Too many certainties have disappeared at the same time, and many are now seeking them from the next world. As God's omnipotence can hardly be reconciled with history's scurviness, a growing number turn to adversarial demiurges. The sects are the secret weapon of the powerless; they want a religion which is not so much opium as crack. The aim seems to be to acquire power which will enable one to combat hostile fate, reassert identity, and obtain revenge. This humus, in which rage and desperation mix with a desire to even scores, nourishes rabid nationalists such as Russia's Vladimir Volfovic Zhirinovsky.

There are positive developments also in former Communist Europe, but episodes of apocalypse postponed are frequent enough to suggest that Christians must not recline in their restored churches. The situation proposes afresh the question raised some years ago by the Polish philosopher Leszek Kołakowski: Did the Church oppose Communism because it was atheist or because it was totalitarian? An implication was: Did the Church defend human rights or was it indifferent to them, interested only in protecting its truths?

Initially, Communist pressure on the Churches—Catholic, Orthodox, and Protestant—was such that they were intent on their own survival rather than being concerned with human rights in general. Only later was this wider concern feasible. Does the answer to Kołakowski's question still affect the choices of Christians today when theoretical atheism has been abandoned but considerable social disorientation exists?

A doctrinal evolution aided Christians to oppose Communism both because it was atheist and because it was totalitarian. John Paul's approach favored this because it did not start from the defense of certain truths only, but also with the human person, whom he called "the way of the Church." John Paul maintained that Jesus reveals not only God to humankind but humankind to itself. He saw atheism as a denial of religious liberty whose affirmation of human transcendence means the individual is superior to political systems. Religious rights thus became the basis of other, related human rights. Those who share these convictions collaborate in favor of all human rights with all those who oppose totalitarianism.

Such collaboration took place in Poland and, to a lesser degree, in Czechoslovakia and Hungary. But even in Poland it became possible on a broad scale only when the Church championed workers' rights. Initially the Catholic Church in Poland felt itself under siege and only in the 1970s took the lead in defending the whole range of human rights. In Ukraine and Romania, after the suppression of the Eastern-rite Catholic Churches, the faithful concentrated all their efforts on ensuring survival. But at the same time in Ukraine a related right was asserted: that of a fully Ukrainian Church. As the Orthodox Church dependent on Moscow became an instrument of Russification, the clandestine Eastern-rite Catholic Church, which used Ukrainian in its ceremonies, was asserting national identity; this was a cause which attracted other civil rights advocates, such as those of the Rukh movement. Obviously, as the Orthodox took over the Eastern-rite Catholic Church, ecumenism suffered. In the Baltic States Christians found in their national identity a bulwark against Communism, but in this case ecumenism was strengthened.

The consequence of these different experiences under Communism is that the post-Communist Catholic Churches in different countries will develop at different speeds; as they have different aspirations, it will be an achievement if they proceed in the same direction. For instance, while some Czech Catholics believe priority should be given to developing collaboration with non-Christians, among seminarians in the former Soviet Union there is a great desire for the whole cloth of the Catholic tradition.

It is affecting to hear a young Albanian engineer recount that his faith was preserved by some lives of the saints and other basic religious books his grandfather gave him even though their possession was a crime. Some Christians in ex-Communist Europe would be entitled to sing not "Faith of Our Fathers" but "Faith of Our Grandfathers" and, even more, "Faith of our Grandmothers". It is one thing, however, to have one's faith nurtured in difficult circumstances by books written at the beginning of the century and quite another, when constraints are no longer imposed, to recoil from what has been written in the past fifty years. In ex-Communist Central and Eastern Europe, John Paul II's inaugural appeal "Be not afraid" should resound again with theology teachers who consider that Rome has succumbed to the modern world's seductions. One said he looked to Poland as the stronghold of sound doctrine, but, as mentioned, in Belarus Father Kotlimowski considers that much of the Polish Church has sold out. Orthodoxy faces a similar or even more acute internal conflict over accepting developments that occurred after the advent of Communism.

Even allowing for the many differences in Central and Eastern European Christianity, the contrast which the philosopher Kołakowski made is not as clear cut as it first appears, because Christian resistance to Communism was always defiance of a totalitarian system and had wider implications. But Kołakowski was right to imply that Christianity was not attractive to outsiders if Christians seemed concerned only with their own interests.

Unfortunately, but perhaps inevitably, since Communism's demise this has been the case to a degree. One reason for the Churches' concentrating on their own interests was that, in states preparing new constitutions and laws, the Churches have been concerned with juridical provisions regarding them. Moreover, to ensure a basis for their institutional life, they have sought the return of confiscated property which, in some cases, was serving a social purpose. They have been preoccupied with obtaining state-run media outlets and state subsidies for their educational and social welfare programs. All this has made them seem unduly concerned with their status, with carving out a niche: as the Churches reinforce themselves institutionally they seem self-absorbed. In addition, the possibility of restoring things can inhibit response to new needs and hinder the flexibility and openness shown by some Christians in the latter years of Communism.

Of course, the problem of witness being in contrast to the institutional Church is not confined to post-Communist Europe, but it is acute there because convincing Christian testimony was so evident in the last years of Communism. The Catholic Church in Poland, for instance, before the collapse of Communism was perceived as serving society as a whole but afterwards was accused of being a pressure group. There was resentment because it was held responsible for faits accomplis such as the introduction of religious instruction in schools, without prior consultation with other denominations, and promoting a concordat with the Holy See. Introduction of a severely restrictive abortion law alienated many. The triumphalistic attitude which provoked a backlash was expressed by an exultant Dominican in Cracow who said, "We've beaten Communism, now we'll trounce liberalism."

In 1991, in a presynodal meeting in the Vatican which John Paul II attended, a Polish priest, Adam Boniecki, issued a sharp warning that "the Church could recover all that was confiscated by Communists, its property, its institutions, its press, and even a political party which sustains it. But at the same time it could lose its most important acquisition in recent years: its credibility [because] each new attempt at discussion within the Church is interpreted as a threat to unity . . . the bishops distrust both criticism and grassroots initiatives."

Boniecki was not heeded in time. Aleksander Kwaśniewski, leader of the ex-Communists who won a relative majority in the September 1993 elections and who succeeded Lech Wałęsa as president in 1995, commented that the Church had lost contact with society because it had chosen to act through laws rather than by shaping people.

Yet Boniecki, who had sounded the alarm, said in 1995 he was "moderately optimistic" that the Church was adapting, that a new generation of leaders was emerging more disposed to dialogue with both believers and nonbelievers and to respect lay initiatives. In fact, late in 1994, the National Council of Lay Catholics, the first formal lay advisory body since World War II, was established by the Polish bishops; the Communists had not permitted lay Catholic associations.

Joseph Tischner has said it was more difficult to believe in God after the French Revolution and more difficult to believe in humankind after the experience of Communism. The antidote to the outlook induced by Communism is not untrammelled market forces because, as Archbishop Miroslav Vlk of Prague complained, "the market sells not only goods but what is more precious: human life." After the drabness of a tragic utopia, the evil of banality menaces ex-Communist Europe. However, certain Christians under Communism confirmed Pascal's saying that "man is infinitely greater than man." The same vision, embodied differently, is still Christianity's best contribution to the dismantlement of walls more resistant than those of Berlin, walls of ethnic hate, religious resentment, and hard-core egoism.

Index

Ch. 1
- Christians behaved & were oppressed diff.   p. 13
- Yet Christianity was the best resource of resistance to totalitarianism.

ch. 2
  - BG: The regime bullied Protestants & catholics but blandished the L
  - RN: A list of the Russian- Orthodox dissidents

* Christian churches helped to preserve & maintain cultural ID
  (Protestant as well)   p. 195, 216
* Positive role of nationalism in UA (p. 198)